PENGUIN PASSNOTES

Across the Barricades

Rosanna Hibbert was educated in schools in the Sudan, Kenya and England. She attended the Guildhall School of Music and was subsequently an educational television producer. She worked on *English File* for the BBC. In one of these programmes a novel by Joan Lingard was featured. Rosanna Hibbert is now a freelance writer.

PENGUIN PASSNOTES

JOAN LINGARD

Across the Barricades

ROSANNA HIBBERT
ADVISORY EDITOR: STEPHEN COOTE, M.A., PH.D.

PENGUIN BOOKS

PENGUIN BOOKS

Published by the Penguin Group
27 Wrights Lane, London, W8 5TZ, England
Viking Penguin Inc., 40 West 23rd Street, New York, New York 10010, USA
Penguin Books Australia Ltd, Ringwood, Victoria, Australia
Penguin Books Canada Ltd, 2801 John Street, Markham, Ontario, Canada L3R 1B4
Penguin Books (NZ) Ltd, 182–190 Wairau Road, Auckland 10, New Zealand

Penguin Books Ltd, Registered Offices: Harmondsworth, Middlesex, England

First published 1988

Made and printed in Great Britain by
Richard Clay Ltd, Bungay, Suffolk
Filmset in Monophoto Ehrhardt

Contents

Acknowledgements   vii
To the Student   ix
Introduction: An Interview with Joan Lingard   1
Summary   5
Commentary   23
Characters   76
Themes   92
Background Information   97
Passages for Comparison   102
Glossary   108

Acknowledgements

For permission to reprint copyright material acknowledgement is made to the following: Denis Campbell and the *Guardian* for an extract from 'A Lesson in Peace Studies', which appeared first on 11 March 1987; Penguin Books Ltd for extracts from Dervla Murphy's *A Place Apart* (Harmondsworth, 1984); Soodlum Music Co. Ltd, Dublin, for 'The Sash My Father Wore' from *Soodlum's Selection of Irish Ballads* (Dublin, 1981); Walton's Musical Instrument Galleries, Dublin, for 'The Wearing of the Green' from *Walton's New Treasury of Irish Songs and Ballads*, Part 1 (Dublin, 1968).

To the Student

The purpose of this book is to help you appreciate Joan Lingard's *Across the Barricades*. It will help you to understand details of the plot. It will also help you to think about the characters, about what the writer is trying to say and how she says it. These things are most important. After all, it is through understanding and responding to plots, characters and ideas that books come alive for us.

You will find this Passnote most useful after you have read *Across the Barricades* through at least once. (Page references are to the Puffin edition.) A first reading will reveal the plot and make you think about the lives of the people it describes and your feelings for them. Then your job will be to make those first impressions clear. You will need to read the book again and ask yourself some questions. What does the writer really mean? What do I think about this incident or that one? How does the writer make such-and-such a character come alive?

This Passnote has been designed to help you do this. It offers you background information. It also asks many questions. You may like to write answers to some of these. Others you can answer in your head. The questions are meant to make you think, feel and respond. As you answer them, you will gain a clearer knowledge of the book and of your own ideas about it. When your thoughts are indeed clear, then you will be able to write confidently because you have made yourself an alert and responsive reader.

Introduction: An Interview with Joan Lingard

Joan Lingard's work room in her Edinburgh apartment is large and high-ceilinged. At one end, by the fireplace, she has comfortable chairs. At the other, backed by tall bookcases, are her desk and word-processor. I filmed her there a few years ago. We sat at a table in the middle of her lovely room and she read passages from her teenage novel *The Gooseberry*. We hid the microphone in a bowl of daffodils.

Ms Lingard is an extremely productive writer. To date (April 1987) she has published ten adult novels and seventeen for young people – and that's not all she has written.

'I started to write for TV in 1970, when I was asked to write for a soap opera called *High Living*.

'I needed to earn some money after my first marriage had broken up. It was great to write for TV; I learnt the ropes. It was a very tight budget: there were a limited number of characters. They rehearsed all week for two episodes and shot them on a Friday afternoon. They didn't do it in short takes but went through each episode without a break, so it was a mad rush changing behind the scenes. I did a subsequent soap for a short time. Then I wrote a number of individual plays; BBC 2 did one on "Play for Today".

'I was asked to adapt my Maggie books for TV and they did that in eighteen parts.'

Joan Lingard has no desire to do any more such dramatizations. 'I've got other work that I'm getting on with. I like to go on to new situations.' Adapting her Maggie books for TV 'was exhausting. I don't really like doing adaptations.'

'I'm asked in schools' (she visits a lot of them, all over Britain) 'if there's going to be a TV adaptation of the Kevin and Sadie books, but no one wants to do that. It seems safer not to; people seem a bit nervy about the idea.' But two stage versions have been written and performed by Theatre in Education companies in various parts of England and Scotland, and the BBC has broadcast a radio dramatization of *Across the Barricades* in Scotland.

Ms Lingard's mother was Scottish, from Edinburgh; her father was English, from London. 'He was the eldest of eleven children, and at fourteen he left home and went to sea in the navy as the lowest of the low, because at home, being the eldest, he had to drag up all ten of his brothers and sisters while my grandmother kept a pub. When I was two we went to Belfast, because my father retired from the navy at forty, as you have to do, and he went into the RNVR and he was sent to Belfast to run a training ship called the *Caroline* and we were there until I was eighteen. So I spent a large part of my life there and was schooled there, and I realize now what that means to a writer. It provides a framework in which to look out at the world. Everything relates back to it; it doesn't mean you're constantly going on about it but it lays down the guidelines.'

What year was it that you left?

'The early fifties. That was when I stopped living there, but I have been back regularly.'

When you left at the age of eighteen, were you conscious of the violence to come?

'One always knew there was an undercurrent going on all the time. There were troubles earlier in the twenties and even into the thirties. My father was not allowed to go up the Falls Road in his naval uniform. There was always this sort of feeling. I was always aware that Catholics were considered "second-class citizens".

'It began as a non-violent civil rights movement in 1968, which then got lost sight of in 1969 when the first flare of violence started up. And actually I was there in 1969 and I can remember the first things were just happening, and people were talking about it with amazement and wondering where it would all lead. No one thought it would lead to the trouble going on – I mean, it's coming up to twenty years now. I think probably everyone was surprised how bitter and how violent it became in the early seventies; the arms, that sort of random violence. To some extent the IRA was thought of as a bit of a joke; they weren't very efficient, especially in the fifties and sixties. It was always said that they would blow their own toes off first before they blew anyone else up. It was also said that they would never put a hand on a woman – they were always safe – and that sort of thing. Of course, it has changed. It's been there, though, all the time; it's been there since 1689. That is why it isn't going away very quickly.'

Is the trouble in Northern Ireland really religious?

'I think politics and religion are deeply intertwined. The troubles are religious, as they are in Lebanon. I think people are inclined to say it isn't, but the religious prejudices bite very deeply in the province' (Northern Ireland) 'and you will find that Protestants have got really deeply ingrained feelings of repugnance against the Catholic church.

'It began because the Protestant forces of King William defeated the Catholic forces of James II in 1689; it was a religious war. It was also political, but then religious wars *are* political too, aren't they? But I would say a lot of trouble is being wrought by people who are not religious.'

It seems to me that Northern Ireland and the Lebanon give religion a very bad name.

'Usually in schools when I'm asked which side I belong to I don't reveal because my aim is to write a completely unbiased account. I think I am successful, because if I go to a Protestant school they think I'm Protestant, and vice versa. That's why I don't say what I am. I have revealed it in an adult novel published in 1984 called *Sisters by Rite*. It's about three sisters growing up in Belfast from the 1940s to the 1970s. They live in the same street, one is Protestant, one is Catholic, and one is a Christian Scientist.'

Are you still a Christian Scientist?

'No – I ceased to be about eighteen years ago. I'm still a believer, but I belong to no established church.'

Do a lot of your books come out of your own life?

'Oh yes, I do think so. That doesn't mean I'm writing an autobiography or anything, but when I read through my books I see the threads that have been taken from my own life, and to a certain extent I think everybody does that. There are all sorts of things in my background that I still have to explore. It's quite a nice feeling because I've now written twenty-six books or something, so I'm really pleased to know that there are seams still to be mined.'

Joan Lingard's seventeenth teenage novel, *The Guilty Party*, is about nuclear power, on which she has strong views. But, she said, 'It's amazing how long something will take before it's ready to emerge. It took Chernobyl to actually move me to write it. Before that I might have done it on nuclear *weapons* only. I've used a lot of my younger daughter's material; she has been arrested and sent to prison many times – a lot of her experiences are in the book.

'I think all the experiences of one's life are there gestating, and you have to be receptive to know when they're ready to come out.'

Once you've started on a book, do you sit here writing a regular number of hours every day till you've finished?

'You need to take time off for a walk or something. I won't sit chained to my desk all day if it doesn't feel right. I work fast, but I have always done a tremendous amount of work in my head beforehand; it has to be there in my head waiting to come out. Ideas for more than one book can be in your head at the same time. I can't see how a blank page can inspire anyone.'

Summary

CHAPTER 1, pp. 5–10

The city: afternoon

Sadie Jackson and Kevin McCoy meet in the home-going rush hour: they haven't seen each other for nearly three years, although they are near neighbours. Walking to a coffee bar, they feel shy, but in the café they unfreeze as they talk about Kevin's sister Brede and Sadie's brother Tommy. They each silently remember (p. 6) how three years ago, when they'd been at their different schools, they'd fought as enemies, had become friends, but that meetings had become too difficult. Kevin says he's working in a scrapyard which is owned by the father of Kate, a girl who used to fancy him. Sadie describes her current job (p. 7) – the third she's had: it's selling hats. She makes Kevin laugh as she describes her customers and says she's thinking of looking for something else.

After they've each hungrily consumed two hamburgers, Kevin suggests that they should go up on Cave Hill (p. 8). On the way to the bus-stop a newspaper billboard catches their eyes, announcing a bomb outrage. Linda Mullet comes up to them at the bus-stop; she's an old schoolfriend of Sadie's. Linda recognizes Kevin (p. 9): he's ... something scandalous. She walks off quickly, and Kevin and Sadie guess she'll soon be spreading gossip. Sadie is rude and funny about Linda.

The bus arrives and the two get on, aware that they are doing a dangerous thing. But they're also ready to enjoy themselves.

CHAPTER 2, pp. 11–18

The Jacksons' house and street: tea-time the same day

Mr Jackson and Tommy await Sadie. They are hungry and per-suade Mrs Jackson to dish up their meal. As they eat (p. 12), Mrs Jackson grumbles about her daughter, Mr Jackson thinks about the Lodge meeting at seven that evening and wishes that Tommy was joining him, and Tommy wonders which film to take Linda to.

Linda walks in (p. 13) and says she doesn't think that Sadie will be coming for her tea. Linda is mysterious and teasing about the person she saw Sadie with. Tommy tries to stop Linda saying any more (p. 14), but she finally brings it out: 'She was with that Catholic boy Kevin McCoy.' This is shocking and disturbing news for Mr and Mrs Jackson (p. 15) and Mrs Jackson has to have some brandy, but both parents think well of Linda for telling them (p. 16).

Tommy and Linda at last go off to the pictures. He is very angry with her for making life difficult for Sadie; he also has to brush away soft memories of Brede, Kevin's sister (p. 17). Linda tries to sweeten the atmosphere. She suggests buying chocolates in Mrs McConkey's shop. The bosomy shopkeeper complains about violence against the troops (p. 18); Tommy tries to reason with her; Linda gets bored. She just wants to enjoy herself; any involvement she's had with the Troubles in the past has been Sadie Jackson's fault, she says to herself.

CHAPTER 3, pp. 19–26

The McCoys' house and street: after tea the same day

Mr and Mrs McCoy and Brede, their eldest daughter (in a family of eight with a ninth due next month), talk about the Troubles and wonder where Kevin has got to. A bang from Uncle Albert's dreadful old car frightens them (p. 20). Has he come to sponge off them again? A band of children appear (p. 21), led by Gerald McCoy and including two more little McCoys, all armed with toy weapons. Mrs McCoy doesn't like such games; she wishes she were back in the green fields of County Tyrone where she was born.

Mr McCoy and Albert drive off to the pub (p. 22). Brede goes down the street to visit Kate Kelly and is 'ambushed' by the children. In Kate's house, next to her father's scrapyard (p. 23), the two remember when they were kids and got into a real fight with Protestants, including Sadie and Tommy. Brede had been badly hurt. Kate wonders if Kevin's got a new girlfriend.

Out in the street (p. 24) there's real trouble; the kids are throwing bricks at two soldiers, and they hit one of them. The soldiers run off. Brede calls Gerald a fool. Big Brian Rafferty, an old friend of Kevin's, says the kids are right (p. 25), but he sends them home. Is he in control of them?

Kate tells Brede that Brian is mixed up with the Provos (the Provisional Irish Republican Army, who believe that violence is necessary). Brede runs home (p. 26), feeling upset and worried, but keeps the kids' doings from her tired, pregnant mother. She waits anxiously for Kevin to come home.

CHAPTER 4, pp. 27–32

Cave Hill and the city centre: the same evening

Sadie and Kevin are sitting at the top of Cave Hill, feeling peaceful and happy together. They agree that they have qualities in common with which their mothers would agree if they met – but of course they never will be able to (p. 28).

The two go hand-in-hand down into the city and into a café for fish and chips (p. 29). Two girls who work in Sadie's store spot her, are introduced to Kevin (p. 30), recognize his name as Catholic and are intrigued. They go, and Sadie asks about Kevin's large family; she is rude about the Pope (p. 31) and they almost quarrel.

Kevin says he'll walk Sadie home – not all the way to her door because that would only cause trouble, but to the end of her street. On their way they are passed by two men being chased by soldiers (p. 32). Their own possible danger makes Kevin and Sadie feel very close.

CHAPTER 5, pp. 33–43

The Jacksons' house and street: later that night

Mrs Jackson is watching television, but Mrs Mullet walks in, so she reluctantly turns the sound down. Her neighbour speculates about Linda and Tommy (p. 34), and tries to stir Mrs Jackson up about Sadie and the Catholic who Linda saw her with. Mr Jackson gets in from his Lodge meeting (p. 35); Mrs Mullet is persuaded to leave.

She overhears Mrs Jackson say how fed up she is with her (p. 36). As the Jacksons discuss Sadie and her 'Mick', Mrs Mullet revengefully decides to spread rumours in the street; she starts straight away with Granny McEvoy (p. 37), but the old woman is too deaf to get the point of the scandal.

Tommy and Linda are in a café after seeing a film. Steve – a schoolfriend of Tommy's and ex-boyfriend of Sadie's – joins them (p. 38). He's become a member of the Lodge and he and Linda reckon Tommy should too. The argument between Linda and Tommy continues in the street – and then they meet Kevin walking Sadie home (p. 39). They exchange tense greetings, Kevin goes (p. 40), the remaining three argue about him and Linda threatens to tell her ma.

As soon as Tommy and Sadie enter their house, Mr and Mrs Jackson rage and storm at their daughter (p. 41). She goes to her room. Tommy puts in some defence of her but does as his parents want, and goes up to Sadie to tell her not to see Kevin again (p. 42).

She reminds him of the good times he, she herself, Kevin and Brede had together three years ago. 'We had to give it up,' he says. Sadie thinks of Kevin as she gets ready for bed.

CHAPTER 6, pp. 44–52

The McCoys' house: the same night

Kevin gets home. A worried Brede meets him upstairs. He tells her his secret – about his meeting with Sadie and his intention to take her to Bangor the following Saturday (p. 45). Brede knows that she can never see Tommy.

The McCoys' street/Mr Kelly's yard/ the Raffertys' house: next day

On his way to work next morning, Kevin runs into Mrs Rafferty and Brian (p. 46), who quizzes Kevin about his patriotism (p. 47). Kevin puts in a long day's work with Mr Kelly – first in the scrapyard (p. 48) and then touring one of the neat, peaceful suburbs, looking for scrap to buy. Brian is sitting in the kitchen when Kevin gets home (p. 49).

As soon as he's finished eating, Brian takes Kevin off to his house (p. 50), and shows him a rifle and ammunition hidden under his bed. Kevin is taken aback and calls Brian a 'nit', which angers him. Brian wants a better hiding-place for the gun and suggests Mr Kelly's scrapyard (p. 51). Kevin says no, Brian calls him a coward, and then tries to get Kevin to 'join us' and fight. Again Kevin refuses (p. 52), saying it's not just the enemy who would die. Brian calls him a traitor.

Kevin promises not to tell anyone about Brian's gun – which Brian then points at him as he leaves the house.

CHAPTER 7, pp. 53–60

Bangor: Saturday

It's a lovely, though windy, day. Being May, Bangor isn't crowded with holiday-makers. Sadie and Kevin walk around the bay to the outdoor swimming pool. She calls him a coward for not joining her in the water; that brings him in (p. 54).

They walk round by the sea and sit on the rocks. At midday (p. 55) they eat all the food Sadie has brought (it was meant to do two meals). They return to the town, and in the amusement arcades Kevin wins first prize in the shooting gallery. He thinks of Brian and his real gun.

They wander on – to the harbour, to tea, and round the bay to the sands at Ballyholme (p. 56). They feel happy. And then they get into an argument about religion (p. 57), made worse by Sadie's stubbornness, and Kevin leaves her.

As Sadie sits there, feeling awful, it starts to rain. She gets soaked – and then Kevin pulls her up and into a shelter (p. 58). She apologizes, so does he, and he kisses her.

They stay in the shelter until the rain stops, go to the bus-station – and miss the last bus home (p. 59). They will have to hitch-hike, which is not easy at night these days.

Kevin and Sadie walk briskly to keep warm, he singing Catholic, she Protestant songs. A noisy, slow car stops for them (p. 60). It's Uncle Albert!

CHAPTER 8, pp. 61–7

On the road from Bangor to Belfast: Saturday night

Uncle Albert's old car stops for Kevin; he and Sadie get in the back. The car then refuses to start (p. 62), so Kevin gets out and gives a push.

They proceed, talking agreeably. Then Kevin and Sadie smell burning rubber, and the engine gives up for good (p. 63). Smoke comes out of the bonnet, so all three get quickly out of the car (p. 64). Uncle Albert's only worry is having his petrol or his (bald) tyres pinched from the vehicle they now walk away from.

They sing as they go: then they come to an army checkpoint; an army car has been blown up and the driver killed. They walk briskly on, but not singing (p. 66).

They get through the suburbs to the little brick terraced streets. They bypass a running battle ahead of them and come to a burning shop. Three o'clock strikes.

Kevin makes sure it's only he who sees Sadie home. They see three men walking towards them – Mr Jackson, Mr Mullet and Tommy (p. 67).

CHAPTER 9, pp. 68–78

The Jacksons' street: Sunday, 3 a.m.

The three men have been looking for Sadie for hours. She refuses to be frog-marched home (p. 69) and is very provocative. Mr Jackson is angry, Mr Mullet backs him up, and Kevin says he doesn't want to fight (p. 70). Mr Mullet calls him a coward. Tommy, who sees no point in fighting, spots two more men approaching, which breaks up the scene (p. 71).

Kevin zigzags through the troubled streets (p. 72). Gunfire sends him sprawling – there is a dead man on the opposite pavement. Kevin is nearly home when Brian Rafferty comes up (p. 73). Brian doesn't like Kevin's distaste for violence: he also threatens Kevin (p. 74); Uncle Albert has told him about his day in Bangor with Sadie.

Various parts of the city: the rest of Sunday

The McCoys go to church. Kate Kelly approaches Brede and Kevin
(p. 75). She tries to date Kevin, fails, and Brede later sees her with
Brian.

After lunch, Kevin goes up to Cave Hill, thinks about Sadie and
gets some sleep. Then he and Sadie meet on the tow path of the River
Lagan (p. 76). They are together till midnight.

Sadie goes to bed smiling with happiness, which worries Mrs Jackson. Kevin, feeling happy too, is attacked by three boys round the side
of the scrapyard (p. 78). He has time to recognize one voice before he
passes out.

CHAPTER 10, pp. 79–87

Brede's day nursery/Sadie's store: Monday afternoon

The end of a working day for Brede. The matron sees her looking
troubled and sends her off early. Brede, desperate to see Sadie, reaches
the department store where she works (p. 80), has to wait for attention
– then learns that Sadie has been sacked (p. 81). She decides that Sadie
must be at home.

Protestant streets/the corner shop/Sadie's house

Brede enters Protestant territory; she is very frightened. She goes into
Mrs McConkey's shop to ask the way. Mrs Mullet is there, and takes
her right to Sadie's door (p. 83). Tommy comes, gets rid of Mrs
Mullet, and fetches Sadie (p. 84).

The café

In the nearby café, Brede tells Sadie about Kevin (p. 85); he is badly wounded. He doesn't know Brede is seeing her; he's all set to keep his appointment with her this evening. Brede insistently asks Sadie not to see him again, ever, otherwise he'll be beaten up again.

Sadie doesn't want to give in to Brian Rafferty and his friends (p. 86), but she likes Brede and sees her point. Brede says, 'There's enough blood, Sadie, without any more getting shed,' and then she leaves (p. 87). What should Sadie do? In twenty minutes she's due to meet Kevin. She leaves the café.

CHAPTER 11, pp. 88–95

By the River Lagan/Mr Blake's house: Monday evening

Kevin walks with difficulty beside the river to meet Sadie. He is terribly weak, but he cannot let her down. He gets to their meeting-place, pretty sure he hasn't been followed because Gerald has checked up on Brian's whereabouts.

An elderly man is walking his dog (p. 89). He's very concerned about Kevin and thinks he shouldn't be out like this. Kevin explains that he's waiting for someone (p. 90). The man says he'll finish his walk, then take Kevin home if his date hasn't turned up.

Man and dog return (p. 91). Kevin knows he's a Protestant, so reveals his Catholicism. The man doesn't mind. He's helping Kevin to the car when Sadie rushes up (p. 92).

She and the man know each other; he's Mr Blake who used to teach her at school. They all get into his car and he drives them to his house in one of the suburbs (p. 93). While he makes coffee and telephones a doctor, Sadie tells Kevin how Brede came to see her for his sake (p. 94); in spite of that, she couldn't bear to let him down this evening.

After a coffee and attention from the doctor, Kevin looks a bit better (p. 95). Sadie says she has decided she must never see him again.

CHAPTER 12, pp. 96–104

Mr Blake's house/Sadie's house and street: Monday evening

Sadie says she doesn't want Kevin to get beaten up again; that's why they mustn't meet. Mr Blake sees them both looking miserable. They all get into his car again (p. 97). Just before Kevin gets out to walk into his own area, Mr Blake invites them both to come to supper on Friday.

Driving Sadie home (p. 98), Mr Blake says she's mad but brave. In the house, Tommy worries that she's seeing Kevin. Sadie tells him she's been sacked from work for keeping company with a Mick, and that her mother is not to know (p. 99).

There is an explosion. Mrs McConkey's shop is burning (p. 100). The Jacksons and Mullets discuss it over a cup of tea. Mrs Mullet and Linda scandalize about Brede's visit to Sadie and the shop (p. 101): did Brede plant gelignite? Mrs Jackson tries to find out why Brede visited Sadie: Sadie won't tell her (p. 102).

Sadie's territory/city centre: Tuesday morning

Going for her bus, Sadie meets Steve and argues about the shop fire (p. 102). On the bus and in the city centre, Linda tries to make friends again. Sadie gets rid of her, then sees a newspaper billboard. Mrs McConkey is dead (p. 103). She feels sick – and decides to go and see Mr Blake (p. 104).

CHAPTER 13, pp. 105–12

Mr Blake's house/the Hendersons' house:
Tuesday morning to Friday evening

Sadie tells Mr Blake about Mrs McConkey and about losing her job.
He offers to pay her to clean and cook for him in the mornings (p.
106). She starts at once, scrubbing and cleaning, and cooking a slightly
spoilt lunch (p. 107). She enjoys the work, to her surprise.

They go for a walk with Jack the dog and meet Mr Blake's neighbour, Moira Henderson, and her children. All of them go back to the
Hendersons' house (p. 108). Sadie admires Moira's paintings (which
she no longer has time for). Mr Blake tells Sadie that Moira is a
Catholic and her husband, Mike, is a Protestant.

Sadie gets home (p. 109). Linda has told the Jacksons about being
sacked; she amazes her mother with news of her new domestic job.

Next morning, while cleaning Mr Blake's windows, Sadie talks to
Moira and offers to look after the children in the afternoons so that
Moira can return to her painting (p. 110). Mrs Jackson is again
amazed, and suspicious about Sadie's happy smile when she thinks
about Kevin (p. 111).

On Friday evening Kevin arrives for supper at Mr Blake's, looking
considerably better. He and Sadie agree that they must keep Mr
Blake's association with them a secret (p. 112).

CHAPTER 14, pp. 113–23

Kevin's territory; Monday, two weeks later

Kevin is not allowed to work: the days seem very long. Mrs Kelly is
chatting with Mrs McCoy; they talk about Kevin, Mrs McCoy defend-
ing him (p. 114). Kevin meets Kate. She tells him his mother has had

a baby girl (p. 116). They have a sticky conversation about Brian Rafferty and finally Kevin gives Kate the brush-off (p. 117).

Brede is at home, coping while her mother is in hospital. She warns Kevin to be wary with Kate; Brede has seen her with Brian (p. 118). Kevin admits he's seeing Sadie. After tea, Brede and her father go off to visit Mrs McCoy.

Sadie's territory: the same day

Sadie is at home for once, being polite to Aunt May (p. 119). Mrs Jackson says Sadie's jobs aren't bringing in enough money; Sadie leaves in a fury and goes to the café (p. 120). Linda and Steve are there. Steve says Sadie's Mick boyfriend is a bad idea. They almost come to blows. Steve knocks over a chair; the café owner makes him pick it up (p. 121). Sadie wanders to the barricades and thinks about Kevin (p. 122).

Kevin's house: the same evening

Kevin's father and sister return from the hospital. Uncle Albert comes in to say that the army is searching the houses in the street; they must have had a tip-off (p. 123). As the soldiers reach the Raffertys' house, Kevin sees Brian coming round the corner.

CHAPTER 15, pp. 124–32

The McCoys' street and house: the same evening

Kevin and Brian stand outside the Raffertys' house while it is being searched. Brian implies that Kevin is an informer. Kevin calls him a coward.

Eventually the soldiers search the McCoys' house – nothing; and the rest of the street – nothing (p. 125). Kevin goes to bed. Just as he's dropping off, the soldiers return. They've come for him (p. 126).

They have found Brian's gun in Kelly's scrapyard. Kevin denies all knowledge of it (p. 127), his family supports him, but the army officer says Kevin was seen with the gun (p. 128). Brede guesses that the witness was Kate (p. 129). Mr McCoy goes with Kevin to the police station.

Brede and Uncle Albert sit up all night. At seven in the morning she runs to the police station and tells the officer that Kate has a grudge against Kevin (p. 130). He asks who she thinks hid the gun: she says nothing. She asks him to keep her visit a secret.

Kevin and his father get home soon after Brede gets back (p. 131). Mr McCoy rages about the army. Kevin goes out. Brede says she's worried that he's going to get his 'framer', who is not Kate (p. 132).

Kevin waits in an alley; Brian Rafferty will come along it on his way to work.

CHAPTER 16, pp. 133–40

Mr Blake's house/Sadie's house: Tuesday

Mr Blake has received a threatening anonymous letter, and it isn't the first. He burns it. The door-bell rings and Kevin tumbles in. There is blood on his shirt – Brian Rafferty's (p. 134). He tries to get his feelings clear: Brian's beating-up was deserved, yet it was stupid.

Sadie arrives. Mr Blake tells her about Kevin (p. 135). Sadie washes the blood out of his shirt while he sleeps, and feels a bit sick. Then she joins Mr Blake, who is weeding his rose bed (p. 136). She worries: is Brian dead? did Kevin have a knife? Mr Blake suggests a trip into the country in the car the next day.

Going home for tea, Sadie meets Tommy carrying a can of turpentine (p. 137). Someone has painted 'A TRAITOR LIVES HERE' on their house. They try to clean it off quickly, but Mr Jackson sees it. Tommy wishes Sadie would stop seeking out Kevin (p. 138).

Sadie's house/the road to Antrim: Wednesday morning

Sadie rises early and cheerful – which makes her mother suspicious. Mr Blake's car is ready. While Sadie is making the picnic lunch, Kevin arrives (p. 139). Brian is not dead, but in bed, he reports. Sadie thinks uneasily of Brian's friends, who are still active.

They load up the car, wave goodbye to Moira and set off for the glens of Antrim (p. 140). The car wobbles. Then it lurches violently across the road. One of the front wheels has come off.

CHAPTER 17, pp. 141–50

The Antrim road/Mr Blake's house: Wednesday and Thursday

The three, plus Jack the dog, are helped out of the crushed car. Mr Blake is very shaken. The police arrive: they'll check with Mr Blake's garage, though he hasn't had a wheel changed for months. An ambulance takes them all to hospital for a check-up (p. 142), and then they get a taxi back to Belfast.

The next morning two plain-clothes policeman interview all three of them. The policeman who does most of the talking reveals that the nuts of *all* the wheels on the car had been loosened. Sadie wonders if Steve wanted to kill her; Kevin thinks about Brian and the other two who beat him up; Mr Blake remembers his four anonymous letters (p. 143).

The policeman asks if they have any enemies: Mr Blake says he hasn't. The officer says a mere hooligan wouldn't have done such a thorough job (p. 144). All three think their secret thoughts again. When the policeman hears Kevin's and Sadie's addresses he's *very* interested (p. 145). He questions them for an hour about their families and friends. Steve and Brian aren't mentioned. He asks about Kevin's bandaged head (p. 146), but Kevin names no one.

Mr Blake goes to his gate with the police. He tells them about the letters he burned. Moira and her children approach (p. 147), and they talk about the success of her 'mixed' marriage to Mike and Mr Blake's desire to help Sadie and Kevin. Back in his house, the couple tell him that, though Sadie will go on working for him, they will meet there less often.

The scrapyard/Kevin's house: Thursday

On his way home, Kevin decides he must not see Sadie again, for her sake (p. 148). He calls at the scrapyard to say he'll be back on Monday. Mr Kelly says he needn't bother, because Kate has said she had seen him with the gun-box. Kevin, furious, tells him he'd better watch the company Kate keeps (p. 149). He tells Brede and his father that he's been sacked.

The city centre: Friday

Kevin goes to the Labour Exchange – no jobs (p. 150). He wishes he could see Sadie and Mr Blake; but he must leave them alone.

CHAPTER 18, pp. 151–61

Sadie's house/Bangor: the days leading up to the 'Twelfth'

For days and days, Sadie wonders why Kevin doesn't phone her at Mr Blake's. At home she hardly goes out, but sits in her bedroom. She hears bands practising for the 'Twelfth'. She tries to imagine what might have happened to Kevin (p. 152).

On the 'Twelfth' all her family go out and the streets are deserted. Sadie goes to Bangor (p. 153), where it rains – and she meets Kevin. They have a wonderful day, except when Kevin says that he might have to leave Belfast to get work (p. 154). They feel right together, but for safety go home on separate buses. They'll meet the following Wednesday.

The McCoys' house: a Wednesday later in the summer

Mr and Mrs McCoy plus three children are about to go in Uncle Albert's car for a week in Tyrone (p. 155). Mrs McCoy fusses over Kevin, who is to be left in charge of the house. Finally the luggage is loaded into the car and they leave. After an imperfectly cooked dinner, Kevin goes to see Sadie at Mr Blake's (p. 157). They have started to meet on Saturdays too, usually in the country. Kevin knows Brede guesses what's going on. This afternoon, Sadie tells him how she avoided taking a job at the butcher's by saying that she always vomited at the sight of blood (p. 158).

Kevin's streets and house/the scrapyard: later that week

Kevin is shopping: there has been rioting the previous night and the street is full of smashed-up shops and other evidence of violence

(p. 159). At the scrapyard Mr Kelly asks him to come back to work. Kevin says he's forgiven Mr Kelly, but no, he wants to leave (p. 160).

Mrs Rafferty teases him about doing the shopping. Kevin gets home and shuts out the street. His restlessness and disgust feel explosive.

CHAPTER 19, pp. 162–8

The Jacksons' house; Friday night and Saturday morning

It is a bad night for fighting: the Jacksons sit up drinking tea. Sadie finally goes to bed, and wakes later than she meant to. She's having a day in the country with Kevin.

Mike Henderson arrives with terrible news (p. 163). Mr Blake's house was petrol-bombed in the night and he is dead (p. 164). The rest of the Jacksons come downstairs. Sadie is weeping. 'It's my fault,' she cries.

Her father gets her a brandy (p. 165). Mike tells them more: no bombers had been seen; this was the first trouble in the district. Sadie remembers that she's due to meet Kevin. Mike understands her dilemma and he and Tommy persuade Mrs Jackson that it'll be all right for her to go. Kevin is waiting happily for Sadie on a sunny bank when she turns up in Mike's car (p. 166).

The Hendersons' house: a few days later

Kevin and Mike go to the funeral; Sadie watches the procession with Moira in her house. She drinks yet another of the many cups of tea and coffee she's been having in the last few long days. Moira looks tired. She's sent the children away and she and Mike have almost had a row about whether or not they too might be bombed (p. 167).

The men return from the service and drink to Mr Blake's memory. Kevin declares that he'll kill the bombers –but later subsides (p. 168): he doesn't want more bloodshed.

He and Sadie walk up on Cave Hill. He tells her he must go. He's not running away, but he's sick of the Troubles. 'It's not living . . .' Sadie is overwhelmed. He's leaving the following week.

CHAPTER 20, pp. 169–74

The McCoys' house and street/the docks: a week later

Brede and Mrs McCoy are packing sandwiches and tea for Kevin on his journey. Mr McCoy is trying to come to terms with his son's departure. Kevin is in his suit, to please his mother. They crack jokes to keep their spirits up (p. 170). Kevin says he may go to London, not stop in Liverpool.

Brede offers to go to the docks (p. 171); Kevin wants her just to walk down the street with him. Mr McCoy produces a fiver. Kevin kisses his mother, who then goes into the kitchen to cry (p. 172). Gerald and the other children are on the pavement. They call and wave as Kevin and Brede walk off. At the end of the street, Brede kisses him and leaves.

By the scrapyard, Kate Kelly apologizes to Kevin about her part in the gun-box incident (p. 173): Brian Rafferty made her lie about it. Kevin suddenly realizes that his old life is over, and begins to feel excited about the new.

Sadie is on the dockside – as Kevin had expected. But she surprises him by saying that she's coming too. She couldn't smuggle out any luggage but she's got her ticket (p. 174).

They go hand-in-hand towards the ship.

Commentary

CHAPTER 1, pp. 5–10

Across the Barricades is the second of five books which Joan Lingard has written about Sadie and Kevin. If you've read the first – *The Twelfth Day of July* – you will need no introduction to Kevin, Sadie and the city they live in. Or will you? How much do you remember about them? If you haven't read the first book, will starting the second one be harder?

Joan Lingard was asked, 'Was it difficult to start writing book two, bearing in mind that there will be some people who haven't read book one?' She replied, 'I didn't really think about it, whether they'd read it or not.' But she has in fact slipped a lot of information about Sadie's and Kevin's past into this first chapter. You can form an opinion about how neatly or otherwise the author has bridged the gap between books. You should also know that she went on to say, 'Of course I had to make *Across the Barricades* entire within itself.'

People

As Kevin and Sadie renew their relationship and bring each other up-to-date they are keeping us informed as well. It is abundantly clear that they are pleased to meet again. What is it about each of them that the other likes? Make lists for each, which you can add to as the book goes on and the characters develop.

A lot of Kevin's reasons for liking Sadie are quite easy to pick up because he tells her several nice things about herself: that she's honest (p. 7); good-looking, can run fast (p. 8); is full of spirit (p. 9). How good are *you* at saying nice things to people? How good are you – or Sadie – at accepting nice things that are said about you? A lot of people, perhaps most of us, find both situations very difficult – and this is not because there's anything nasty about us. Try giving and receiving true compliments with your friends. If you try it more than once, the experience will become easier to cope with and you may discover a quality that Kevin seems to have had all along. Do you feel it's the gift of the gab, honesty, wanting to please, confidence, generosity . . .? What does it take to *accept* compliments? Vanity, honesty, wanting to please, confidence . . .? Has Sadie got it?

One thing she certainly has got which is very attractive is a sense of humour. Watch out for it all through the book. She hasn't got complete control over it, which makes life a bit tricky at times.

Seven other main characters are introduced in this chapter: Sadie's mother, Mrs Jackson (pp. 5 and 7); Brede, Tommy, Kate and her father (p. 6); Linda Mullet (p. 8); her mother, Mrs Mullet (p. 9). Only one of them – Linda – plays a direct part in the chapter; the others are all introduced in other ways.

Here are some possible ways of bringing in new characters, and telling your readers something about them:

- The author names/describes them in the narration.
- An established character talks about them.
- An established character thinks about them.
- The author or an established character quotes things they have said.
- They are written about in a newspaper or letter.
- A letter they themselves have written is read by an established character.
- Someone writes a letter to them.
- Someone imitates them.
- Someone tells jokes about them.
- Someone dreams about them.

There are so many ways to bring in new characters, and some of these are so adaptable and lively that it would be quite possible to have people in stories who (unlike Linda on p. 8) never actually put in an appearance and yet seem as real and important to us as if they did.

You might like to try writing a story, or part of one, bringing in characters in different ways. First look carefully at how Joan Lingard has done it in Chapter 1, and use the list of possibilities above. The author has a very sharp eye, a strong sense of humour and a way of writing which doesn't waste words. That's a lot to match up to. But it's worth trying.

The more you are aware of an author's skills – and trying to copy them is a good way of training your awareness – the more enjoyment it is possible to get out of their work. It is, of course, the mark of a good writer that we can get pleasure from reading them *without* pulling their books to pieces. But if we can approach writing more closely by trying to understand a bit about technique, we can certainly increase the quality of our enjoyment.

Place

Throughout this chapter we are given clues – some dramatic, some more subtle – about the setting for the book. On the very first page, line 3, we have: 'The pavement was thick with people heading homewards.' What does this tell you? Look for more references to the city and what is going on in it. How many can you find?

Politics

Twice in this chapter (on pp. 7 and 8) Kevin and Sadie find it impossible to think or talk directly about the violence in the city. Can you think of reasons for this? Are you sympathetic towards them in this difficulty? Or are they just burying their heads in the sand?

Look at lines 14 and 15 on p. 5. It would be worth memorizing this sentence: it rings true in many other chapters. Now look at the paragraph on p. 6 beginning, 'They were silent for a moment . . .' and the paragraph that begins on the last line of p. 9. Hold these in your mind too as you read on into the story: the whole book is based on difficulties and dangers and how different people react to them.

CHAPTER 2, pp. 11–18

On one level, pp. 11 and 12 give an excellent description of hungry people wanting, then getting, a delicious fry-up, with a brilliant four-line sketch thrown in of the way Sadie's mother treats her hair (note the use of the word 'garnished' in line 2, p. 12). But fun though this is, there are a lot of important things going on. Look for and make notes about:

1. leads to Sadie's character in what her family say about her;
2. clues about Tommy's relationship with Sadie;
3. the importance, particularly to Mr Jackson, of Protestanism and its symbols (the Lodge, the Orange Walk, the Twelfth of July: see 'Background Information' and 'Passages for Comparison');
4. how the men treat Mrs Jackson;
5. what Tommy's job is.

On p. 12, ten lines up from the bottom, Mrs Jackson complains about someone, and Tommy leaps to her defence. Who are they talking about? Who have we all been thinking about most on these two pages?

Look at the first line on p. 13: 'They heard the front door opening . . .' In comes not a member of the family, but Linda Mullet. What does this tell you about life in the Jacksons' street? Could the same sort of thing happen where you live?

The strands of character and plot in this chapter are woven in a more complicated pattern from now on. So first read pp. 13 to 18 without stopping before we try to unravel the strands.

Look at Linda first. What is she up to on pp. 13–16 until she leaves the house with Tommy? Can you think why she's so keen to do Sadie a bad turn? (Look at the last sentence on p. 18.)

In three and a half pages, Linda uses various parts of her body on at least twelve occasions to control how others react to her. In other words, she's using *body language* (combining it with words, of course). If the others had been cleverer at spotting her tactics, she might not have had the results she wanted. Quite a lot of jobs need body language/interpreting skills: for example parenting, teaching, social work, dancing, acting. Which of these might Linda be good at? Can you spot how, alone with Tommy, she goes on getting her way by using the same techniques? Note that she also lies to win her points, but that when she lies to Tommy she isn't always so successful.

She must be careful with Tommy: she's sharp enough to see that Brede means something special to him, but confident enough to make an extremely objectionable remark about her in the middle of p. 17. (Perhaps most of us need to replace the abusive religious word 'Mick' with an abusive racial word to see just how painful and disgusting Linda's remark is.) What do you think of Tommy's reaction?

On the whole, Tommy comes out of this chapter pretty well. From the bottom of p. 13 onwards he tries to stop Linda in her tracks. For why he does this, look again at your reactions to his behaviour on pp. 11 and 12.

Now look at Mr Jackson's thought on p. 12 about Tommy being 'a good Protestant' and Tommy's thoughts about Brede (who is a Catholic, remember) – both guessed at by Linda (and you?) at the top of p. 15, and described quite fully in the second half of p. 17. Contrast Tommy's 'no point in thinking of her' with his sister's positive relationship with a Catholic. Does this tie up with line 11 on p. 17: 'He was usually very peaceable, much more so than Sadie'? Look carefully at all his words and thoughts about Brede: he certainly likes the thought of her – but how intensely, do you think?

Before we leave Tommy in this chapter, re-read his conversation with Mrs McConkey on p. 18.

From what you know of Tommy so far, which of these descriptions would you underline as being accurate about him?

stubborn	perceptive
loyal	steady
shallow	a soft touch
narrow-minded	caring
weak	rough
strong	gentle
honest	rude

Underline as many as you think right, even if some contradict others. Add more descriptions if you want to.

Mr and Mrs Jackson are both very concerned about Sadie's relationship with a Catholic. It's 'a desperate shock', and the thought of marriage brings on the need for brandy. You may discover more about their feelings for their daughter as the book goes on; but so far, what do you think they are? Remember Mrs Jackson's grumbles before and at tea; notice exactly when Mr Jackson starts to pay real attention (on p. 13). Are Sadie's parents influenced by religious prejudice? Or loving? Are they only interested in their own reputations? Bewildered by Sadie's lively originality? Proud of her?

Now to a point about writing. Note two high spots of humour: the one about Mrs Jackson's rollers, and Sadie's joke about Mrs McConkey's vast and growing bosom. We can all – and all too easily – make jokes about other people's appearance; but can you do it with style and affection, as Joan Lingard and her characters do here? Try it!

Finally, having unravelled the threads in this chapter, go back to p. 11 and re-read it through non-stop as one woven piece.

CHAPTER 3, pp. 19–26

This chapter doesn't push the plot along very far, but nevertheless it is full of incident and – more importantly – of characters and atmosphere.

Firstly, it balances the Protestantism of Chapter 2; it is our first 'Catholic' chapter. This gives it quite a different colour, as it were. Look at this list of Catholic/political views, mark the page numbers on which they appear, then turn back to Chapter 2 and see if you can find their Protestant equivalent:

Page

Mr McCoy resents house searches.
He thinks the British should get out.
He says the kids playing 'Provo' games is normal.
Uncle Albert encourages Gerald and his crowd.
Brian Rafferty has got mixed up with the Provos.
He thinks little Gerald is 'fighting for his country'.
He approves of this.
What's more, he seems to be in control of the kids.
Mrs McCoy worries when Kevin is out late.

She worries when little kids taunt soldiers.
She doesn't like the kids' violent games.
She isn't pro-Protestant.
But she doesn't see the need for street fighting.
Brede thinks the British army might possibly be useful.
The fact that they're in Belfast is not their fault.
The kids' war games worry her.
She calls Gerald a fool for throwing stones.
Brian's attitude makes her sick.
Kate thinks the kids are just being kids.
She's not interested in Brede's and Brian's political
  argument.

What political/religious views and actions can you find among the Protestants in Chapter 2? Do they correspond with the ones here in quantity, depth of feeling or balance? Are they, for instance, as anti-British?

It's probably true to say that, with most people, the views they hold show us a lot about their character. This chapter brings a lot of new people into the story. As you think about the way they see the world, you will learn a lot about the kind of people they are. Kate and Brian are going to play very important parts in the plot later on: can you jot down ways in which you think they might act? What about Brede? She seems to be a more complicated person; can you guess what sort of part she might play? Do you see her so far as a bit of a po-faced spoilsport? A strong, calm person? Or what?

Of all the new characters in this chapter, which appeal to you most? Write down what you like about them.

Violence

There will be a lot of violence in this book – that's inevitable in a story about Catholics and Protestants 'mixing it' (in any sense) in Belfast in modern times. We've already had reported violence on pp. 8 and 17–18; memories of a fight on pp. 6 and 14 (which Brede remembers in this chapter, p. 23); evidence of street fighting on p. 7.

But now we get, first, children disturbingly practising for a fight (note how well they've observed the real thing: see the first two lines of p. 22), and then the reality of stones and other missiles, a bloody head and two powerless, frightened (or prudent?) soldiers.

We also have the perhaps equally frightening verbal violence – shouts of 'Coward!' and 'Traitor!'. Remember them and note where they come; you will hear them again.

Lastly, after all these serious things, don't miss the funny, gentle or melancholy passages. Look at the second half of p. 20 and Mrs McCoy's dream of County Tyrone on p. 21. Can you find more? And now decide: is there really room for these relaxed moments in a serious chapter? Do you like Joan Lingard's intermittent flashes of humour?

CHAPTER 4, pp. 27–32

(*a*) At last we are back with Sadie and Kevin in person, rather than in other people's conversations or thoughts. Have you *missed* them, or felt *annoyed* by not knowing what they were doing? Or have you been waiting with *excitement* or *pleasant anticipation* to catch up with them? Underline whichever words in italics apply to you. Or think of other words to describe your reaction.

(*b*) What does this say about Joan Lingard's method of constructing this novel? Has she been *keeping you interested*? *Frustrating* you? Again underline any italicized words you think relevant; or think of some of your own to describe how you feel the book has treated you so far.

Notice how your response to paragraph (*a*) has helped to give meaning and reason to your response to paragraph (*b*). When giving opinions or judgements, by all means make them personal – but do try to back them up with reasons which show that you have thought about them first. (This is useful in real life as well as in exam papers!)

This chapter is very largely about Kevin and Sadie's growing relationship. They are at peace in the evening up on Cave Hill. The author has written a (for her, rare) purely descriptive paragraph to start the chapter. It beautifully sets the mood, and places the two young people literally and emotionally above the trouble in Belfast.

The last paragraph on p. 27 describes Kevin for us and on the next page we're given one of the most important reasons why he and Sadie get on so well. This is confirmed by Kevin half-way down p. 28 when he speaks of how their mothers talk about each of them. (See also lines 20 and 21 on p. 6, and p. 10.) What is this bond? Add it to the list of 'likes' you started making in your work on Chapter 1. From your experience and observation, do you think it's a good basis for a close relationship?

Kevin and Sadie touch each other quite a lot in these few pages. Do you think that 'real people' would do this so early in a relationship? Would you, for instance? Talk about it with your friends. And write down what you think this gentle, perhaps slightly shy, kind of contact does for the two people. What does it do for the reader?

Look at the two sentences starting six lines from the bottom of p. 28, and lines 10–11 on p. 29. If you like them, try writing just one or two short sentences about Kevin and Sadie touching each other to go somewhere else in this chapter – perhaps at the start, on Cave Hill; perhaps in the café after they've made up their quarrel. Try to keep the right mood for the moment you've chosen. Do you like what you've written? Was it hard or easy to do?

Before we leave Cave Hill, look on p. 28 for two short consecutive sentences which seem to tell us that Sadie is actually falling in love. (They are on the second half of the page.)

Most of pp. 29 and 30 are taken up with the encounter with the two girls from Sadie's store. No doubt you recognize their reaction to the Protestant/Catholic 'mix'. (Refer back to Linda on p. 9, and Linda and the Jacksons in Chapter 2.)

When the two girls go out, Sadie laughs at them: 'They've got something to talk about . . .' she says. Kevin is disgusted at the gossip. Re-read the first paragraph on p. 30. Now – do you feel amusement and disgust is all the two young people feel? Might they also be feeling something else?

fear
apprehension
anger

'Oh, God, how boring!'
'Bet they wouldn't have the nerve to do what I'm doing!'

Are any of these emotions worth underlining?

Here we come to an important piece of dialogue, beginning on p. 30, in which Sadie asks Kevin about his family and is rude and silly about his religion. He is rude back. Write a list of the things this scene tells us about each of them. (Some are spelt out for us by Joan Lingard; others you must look for yourself.) What is the value of this quarrel to Sadie and Kevin?

The scene ends when Kevin says, 'I wouldn't have nine kids myself, mind you.' Do you think that the reason he goes on to give is true? Or the only one? How does it tie up with the last three lines on p. 30 and the first three on p. 31?

Have you got views on the virtues or otherwise of having – or being a member of – a large family? Could you write, say, 150 words about this? (Some points which might be useful: emotional support between siblings;* favouritism; learning to put a value on yourself; hard work; physical effect; economics; economic and emotional support of parents; religious/cultural background.)

A note on tolerance, or rather the lack of it. On p. 31 Kevin and Sadie say stupid things to each other about their religious beliefs. When even these two – who are as broad-minded as almost anyone else in the novel – can say things like that, you can see how strong the pull of prejudice can be.

It would almost be worth learning p. 32 by heart; it's certainly worth reading aloud, preferably to an audience. It has warmth, love, danger and harshness, and a challenge – all in 118 words. The hunted men and the chase are described in 55 words. Try to think of an action-packed, short, dangerous or threatening incident and give yourself 75 words to describe it. You will learn something about economical writing, and how good at it Joan Lingard is. And – just to keep you humble! – consider that in this chapter's four and a half pages she has taken us from lyrical peace, through growing love, laughter, a good meal, an edgy encounter, a serious quarrel and a horrible moment, to strength and closeness.

* If you don't know what this means, go to a good dictionary: it's a pleasant and useful word.

CHAPTER 5, pp. 33–43

A quick memory test. Describe the significant thing about Mrs Jackson's appearance as she watches T V.*

The first five pages of this chapter confirm Mrs Mullet as a trouble-maker. Jot down other aspects of her character which are evident here (look at description, dialogue, Mrs Jackson's thoughts) and find a word or two to describe her relationship with Mr Jackson. Use up to line 15 on p. 36 for this exercise. (By the way, 'dry bokes' is a very strong expresson; it means retching – which you do when you want to be sick but have nothing to bring up as vomit; in other words, something extremely unpleasant.)

Taking in the narrative up to the top of p. 37, look at Mr and Mrs Jackson's *attitude to Sadie and her doings*. Remember that at this stage they only have hearsay evidence. Underline any of the following words if you think they describe either of them:

defensive	protective
distressed	suspicious
caring	hopeful
worried	resentful
trusting	violent
furious	

As well as everything else, the first scene on these pages, up to Mrs Mullet's exit, is quite funny – partly because of the writing (including the dialogue), partly because of Mrs Jackson's splendidly controlled use of her 'props' (short for 'properties': inanimate objects used by actors). If you re-wrote this scene as a radio script, making sure you included all the sound-effects, its humour would become very obvious and rather fun to perform.

The last paragraph on p. 36 has a high political content. Look at your work on Chapter 3: how many more parallels does this passage here add to the Catholic ideas and activities there? What about the four small boys in this paragraph, for example?

A final note before we move on: did Mrs Mullet's easy access to her neighbour's house remind you of the top line of p. 13, by any chance?

In the café. Can you remember Tommy's attitude to Linda as they

* If your memory needs rescuing, turn to p. 12.

set off to the cinema (pp. 16–17)? It seems to have changed at the bottom of p. 37. Can you see why?

Steve is yet another person to put pressure on Tommy to behave like 'most of the men round here'. (See p. 12.) If you have not read *The Twelfth Day of July*, you may not fully understand Tommy's reason for not taking part in Orange ceremonial. Your school or local library is bound to have a copy.

Tommy has strong views (see lines 9–6 from the bottom of p. 38), but he doesn't want to talk politics – and what's the result? Steve implies (lines 2–3, p. 39) that he's afraid, Linda (lines 6–7) that he's weak. Has the same sort of thing happened to you or anyone you know? There's an expression, 'the strong, silent type' (which Tommy happens to be); a lot of people can't stand others' silence, and hit back with damaging comments.

The encounter with Kevin and Sadie on pp. 39–40 is brief because Kevin has the sense to go quickly, but Linda makes as much of it as she dares and it is now quite clear that she and her mother are tarred with the same scandalmongering brush. Sadie's quick temper doesn't help, of course. Tommy thinks that she has the devil in her at times; does that ring a bell? (See p. 28.) What is Sadie's excuse for her outburst?

When the storm breaks in the Jackson house, how do you think Sadie stands up to her parents? Which of them handles Sadie better? Go back to the list of adjectives about their attitude to their daughter and see if you want to underline any more of them.

Upstairs, Sadie has a very important conversation with Tommy (p. 42). She has quietened down and speaks with a lot of maturity. Pick out and write down what you think is the most important thing she says.

The last five lines of dialogue on that page are very important in that they continue the plea for tolerance which runs through the book. Sadie wonders if, as children, they should have gone on trying to overcome the barriers of prejudice. Tommy doesn't think personal efforts like that make any difference. Do you agree with either view? There is a saying from the Women's Movement: 'The personal is political.' Sadie might agree. But it's hard to get one's own thoughts clear on important issues like this. Talking – or, perhaps more likely, arguing – about it helps a lot. Then you might feel clear enough in your mind to write three or four paragraphs to back up either Tommy or Sadie.

CHAPTER 6, pp. 44–52

Before you start, we can consider a question of age. We have only just been told *how old Sadie and Kevin are* (on pp. 41 and 44). Did you mind not being told this earlier? Had you guessed? Does age matter in books . . . in real life? However you've replied to the last question, jot down a few reasons to support your answer – and check with some older people to see if they agree with you.

It is typical of Brede that she stays awake until her brother comes home. She is doing the worrying for her mother (see the first paragraph on p. 46 for something else that Brede shares with her mother) and for herself, and twice on p. 44 we are given the reason why caring families should worry about young men in Belfast.

Read the whole of Brede and Kevin's dialogue on pp. 44–5. What about Kevin's reaction to seeing Brede waiting up for him? Is he:

surprised
fed-up
pleased
expecting it?

Have you any other, better words for this?

Look at the last paragraph on p. 45. Can you write a dialogue between Brede and yourself, trying to persuade her that if she wants to see Tommy she should jolly well try to? To do this, you could play the part of a caring friend, a trouble-maker, or someone who believes that 'the personal is political'. (See 'Commentary' for Chapter 5.)

The McCoys' house (see p. 45). Where is Mr and Mrs McCoy's bedroom? Can you explain this?

Brian Rafferty isn't a difficult character to understand. We've already learned (at the bottom of p. 25) that 'he's got himself mixed up with the Provos' and that he's big and a fighter. In this chapter we are given confirmation of all this, plus evidence of a quick temper. Why do you think he's trying to recruit Kevin to his views? Why, when Kevin proves stubborn, does Brian become not only angry but deeply, woundingly offensive? ('Coward' (p. 51) and 'traitor' (p. 52) are very damaging terms.)

Do you think that any or some of these sentences are right:

- He's a true believer in the need for violence.
- He wants to recruit lots of people to the Provos.
- He's active and physical.
- He's not very bright.
- He doesn't like being disagreed with because he knows he's right.
- He doesn't like being disagreed with because he doesn't like arguments.
- He's brave.
- He's a patriot.

Kevin's attitude to Brian is more subtle and less assured than Brian's to Kevin. He says 'Brian's all right' on p. 48, but is 'not at all sure' on p. 49. The paragraph beginning at the last line of p. 46 shows Kevin's doubts very clearly. (See also the first two lines of p. 52.) The paragraph implies that Kevin has changed over the years, while Brian hasn't. This bothers Kevin. Have you too had friends in the past in whom you no longer feel so interested? Does this bother you? Should it?

Friendship often works the other way, of course: you might know someone for ages before you realized – or decided – that you could be true friends with them. It would be interesting, and perhaps very funny too, to discuss with your friends how you all feel about each other now compared with in the past, and why this is.

The rifle. Once Brian has revealed the gun (on p. 50), Kevin has to do two things. What is the first? (See the first half of p. 51.) What is the second? (Two key lines are: 'There's enough people getting killed', and 'There's dozens of Catholics who aren't one of you . . .')

This whole scene, from p. 50 onwards, is an important turning-point. You may well want to refer to it in exam answers, so be sure that you remember where in the novel it comes.

We have missed out Kevin at work with Mr Kelly (pp. 48–9). You need to remember that Mr Kelly is the father of Kate – who is presumed to be Kevin's girlfriend (pp. 6 and 23).

There are two linked points to get out of these pages. The first is the description of the suburb Mr Kelly drives to in his search for scrap. It is peaceful and therefore utterly unlike Kevin's street (and Sadie's, for that matter). The second point is Kevin's reaction to this peacefulness. The key lines are the last two on p. 48 and the first two on p. 49.

Can you explain why Kevin 'could not see himself anywhere'? Is it that's he growing up and changing? Is it to do with Sadie? As a matter of interest, turn back (to p. 42), where Sadie says, 'I'm sick of this street and all the people in it.' Is this yet another example of the two of them being amazingly alike? (See 'Commentary' and your work on Chapter 4.)

Cross-Referencing

For once, look at how this 'Commentary' is written; the paragraph above, for instance, has two cross-references in it (in brackets). They are there to help you collect information. Cross-referencing may make you cross, because you're forever flipping backwards and forwards through the pages of the novel, these *Passnotes* or your own work; but do try it, because it does help you to get to know *Across the Barricades* really well. If you take cross-referencing slowly and calmly, you might even start to enjoy it – and find more of your own to indulge in. All good and interesting books, fiction and factual, are goldmines for keen cross-referencers.

CHAPTER 7, pp. 53–60

Kevin and Sadie have set out to have a really good day together in a seaside town, Bangor, which they both like, and up to their quarrel (on pp. 56–7) they succeed wonderfully. (Kevin's memory of Brian and his rifle is the only momentary disturbance.) Go through pp. 53–6 and note down the various ways the couple's enjoyment is shown. Is it:

- in the narrative writing? Give examples.
- in the dialogue? Give examples.
- in the descriptive writing? Give examples.

Do you like the way in which Joan Lingard has expressed Kevin's and Sadie's happiness?

As you are doing this exercise, you will come across three other things. The first is on p. 54 – the cold swim in the Pickie Pool. How does Sadie get Kevin into the water? How does Kevin's reaction compare with his response to Brian on p. 51, six lines from the bottom?

The second extra thing arises on p. 55. Sadie notices that she and Kevin 'kept finding things on which they agreed, attitudes they shared'. This should have rung a loud bell with you by now. It would be encouraging, too, if you knew where to look back to for cross-references on this point. The third extra thing has actually got a name:

Sexual Stereotyping

The term means taking traditional, accepted attitudes of females and males and re-using them, in thought or action, without input from your own mind or experience, or from more modern ideas.

The examples here start on the bottom line of p. 54; Kevin – quite unthinkingly – 'knows' that girls can't skim stones nearly as well as boys can. Sadie has a sharp, modern response. But she herself falls into the stereotyping trap in the next line. Can you see how? Is her excuse, 'I like my grub', the only reason why she brought the picnic? Is there anyone else around who might have thought about bringing food? How does he try to show that *he* can look after *her*? By offering to do the 'male' thing: to *buy* the next meal.

Notice, by the way, that it isn't only males who do the stereotyping. Sadie here has stereotyped herself as 'caring woman' by bringing food, and 'economically weak woman' by letting Kevin pay for her meal (on this particular day and in the past). She has also, of course, agreed with Kevin's stereotyping of himself as 'economically strong male'.

This is quite complicated, isn't it? But it's worth disentangling. You might get it clear by thinking of a similar incident between a female and a male, of any age, and trying to write it so that one of them does or says completely non-stereotypical things and the other reacts in an absolutely traditional way. Choose an ordinary event such as:

  shopping
  driving somewhere
  going to the cinema
  feeling hungry
  feeling ill

Get other people to read what you've written. They may spot stereotyping that you've missed. How do they like your revolutionary scenario?

There is a lot of sexual stereotyping in this novel, for example in the way the men at home sit around waiting for their women to dish out food to them. But if there were not any stereotyping, what would happen to the novel? Would it lose a lot of its truth? Whether we like it or not, stereotyping and sexism are everywhere; so, whether *she* likes it or not, Joan Lingard, who is an acute observer of human beings, puts it in her books.

The quarrel and its consequences. In Chapter 4, p. 31, Sadie is very insulting to and about Kevin's religious beliefs. Here, on pp. 56–7, she pushes her luck too far and drives Kevin away. Religion is a notoriously difficult subject to argue about quietly. Sadie knows this ('Give over, a voice inside her was saying'). Why on earth does she go on so? Is she:

  stupid
  insensitive
  fascinated by Catholicism
  frightened by Catholicism
  wanting to provoke Kevin
  or what?

Whatever her reasons,* her behaviour is pretty childish. All the more credit to her, then, that she apologizes fully to Kevin. (Most of us know how dreadfully difficult that can be; impossible sometimes.)

  * In the next book, *Into Exile*, Sadie still has trouble coming to terms with Kevin's Roman Catholicism.

Kevin is very generous in the way he accepts Sadie's being sorry. (It's not always easy to do that either.) Altogether, the result of the quarrel is a warm, loving scene, ending with a kiss, and bringing back happiness to the day – in spite of missing the last bus home.

Kevin and Sadie have moved another step closer to each other. Indeed (on p. 59) they can even sing political songs to each other which, when they were quarrelling, would just have added fuel to the fire. Even if you don't know the songs, you can guess the significance of each one to the person who is singing it.* Do you know any other religious, political or nationalistic songs? What's the reason for singing them? Are football songs and chants part of the same thing?

On p. 59, in the paragraph beginning, 'They set out on the road', can you explain why drivers are unwilling to give lifts at night?

Again on p. 59, look at the short paragraph beginning, 'It chugged towards them.' What's clever about this writing? It's very descriptive. It's full of action. Do you see? Yes – short sentences can be very useful. Try writing a scene of action and/or emotion where short sentences will help the mood. They must be *proper* ones, with subject, object and verb.

CHAPTER 8, pp. 61–7

This is a short chapter, and on the whole a merry one. It is hardly more eventful than the last – which does not mean that it is insignificant; Joan Lingard isn't going to *waste* six pages. Chapters 7 and 8 between them recount the last time that Kevin and Sadie can feel truly relaxed and uninvolved personally in the Troubles; and this chapter is the last extended comedy scene that we have in the book.

Joan Lingard has said, '*I really believe in having humour in a book because it's part of life, and it lights up even the sombre parts. I myself enjoyed Uncle Albert. I needed him to come on.*'

So let's enjoy Uncle Albert's big scene, noting as we read his sympathetic attitude to youthful romance (pp. 61 and 66), his ready

* The words of the songs are included in 'Background Information', pp. 97–101.

liking of Sadie, and his acceptance of the disaster with his car (p. 63: 'there's always a bit of a smell . . .', and p. 64: 'Uncle Albert always had friends who could fix things . . .').

Write down other aspects of Uncle Albert's personality and say whether you like them or approve of his attitude. Don't miss what Kevin thinks about him on p. 62, who starts the singing on p. 65, or what Sadie and Kevin say about him on p. 67. (See also p. 20.) What about Uncle Albert's political views: do you think they're extreme? Moderate? Surprising? Who else is 'not for people getting killed'?

Do you, like Joan Lingard, enjoy Uncle Albert? If there's anyone in real life whom you enjoy in the same way, try writing a short description of them, or the story of something they've done. If you can't think of a person, are there any animals who have made you laugh? Write with as much humour and affection as you can, as Joan Lingard does. (An important thing to know about writing comedy is that you will not give pleasure and understanding to your readers if you simply get us to laugh *at* a character: *you must have us laughing with them.*) If you think that writing comedy sounds too difficult, try *telling* the story to friends or family and see what reaction you get – but stick to the 'rules': keep it short and keep it affectionate.

The serious passages in the chapter are mostly to do with the violence outside and in the city. They are all economical with words. In particular, the paragraph on p. 66 beginning 'They did not sing any more' is a marvellously vivid short description of Belfast.

The encounter on p. 67 is written about much more fully than the other troubled meetings and street events in the chapter. Is this because:

● Joan Lingard has lost control of her writing?
● it is the most dramatic event in the chapter?
● it's important to the plot?
● we must be made to stop enjoying Uncle Albert and get down to the nitty-gritty?

Tick one or more of the suggestions, or find one of your own.
Finally, why are Sadie's family so concerned about her that they

send out a search party? She's always been pretty independent, surely? *

CHAPTER 9, pp. 68–78

Having said a fond farewell to comedy, here it comes again in the not very impressive shape of Mr Mullet. The first scene is serious and important, but Linda's father, with his blundering, rather fear-full presence, is very amusing. Write down more words to describe him: why have you chosen them?

Do you like the mixture of humorous and serious moods? It's to be found all through the book, isn't it? For instance, any scene in which Sadie appears is likely to have a strong spark of humour. For the big scenes, where the mixture is particularly noticeable, look again at Chapters 2 and 5.

Chapter 9 is full of meetings, several of which are dramatic enough to be called encounters. To give yourself a quick guide to events, complete this list:

People meeting	*Religious loyalty*	*Place*
1.		
2. Kevin/police	Catholic/neutral	Catholic street
3.		
4.		
5. Kevin/family	Catholic/Catholic	Catholic church/ street
6.		
7. Kate/Brian	Catholic/Catholic	Catholic street
8.		
9.		
10. Mr and Mrs Jackson	Protestant/Protestant	Home
11.		

Meeting no. 1 (pp. 68–7). We see more of *Mr Jackson's* character than we have before. Find and write down what we learn about him.

* The answer is on p. 41.

Have you words to describe him? *Tommy* is confirmed as a basically peaceable, sensible young man, far more understanding of Sadie's fieriness than her father is. Who else tries to keep Sadie quiet?

There is a *sixth, invisible person* in this encounter. Who is it? Why are Mr Jackson and Mr Mullet concerned with this person? Have you noticed that their thoughts and words about the 'invisible sixth' form a strong thread in the comedy woven into this scene?

For the third chapter running, Kevin is called a coward. Why does he always rise to the bait – even when Sadie uses the word as a joke? Is it for any of the following reasons?

● He likes fighting back.
● He hates being called rude names.
● He is not a coward.
● He's a bit of a coward and wants to hide it.
● He doesn't like people who use the word.
● He isn't sure how brave he is, and wants to make up his own mind.
● He hasn't got a sense of humour.

You may want to tick more than one of these, or add others.

After this come more vivid, economically written scenes set in the Belfast streets (pp. 72–3). Read *the machine-gunning scene*. How might it be shown on T V or in a film? Write a film script, putting in descriptions – or drawings – of the pictures you'd shoot. Now compare your version with Joan Lingard's. Have you put in:

the gunman
other extra characters
extra words
mess and debris in the street
ruined buildings
blood?

Would you let your 8- and 9-year-old sister or brother see your film?

Kevin and Brian (pp. 73–4). What do you think of Brian 'grinning' about the night of violence? Is he being patriotic? Have you any other words for him? Does he really believe that the Prods would 'burn us out to the last man'? If so, give his reasons. (Does Brian visualize *women* being burned out by the Prods? Perhaps – like most people – he reckons the word 'man' stands for 'all humans'; perhaps he doesn't think women come into this at all. Either way, have another look at the notes on sexual stereotyping in the Commentary for Chapter 7.)

Uncle Albert has blabbed about Kevin and Sadie to Brian. Who else in this novel tells tales – or rumours – out of turn? What is Joan Lingard's reason for having these people in the book?

Useful hint. You should try to remember when in the book, and why, Kate and Brian get their heads together.

Kevin and Sadie (pp. 76–7). They have a few happy hours together in a neutral and attractive part of Belfast. Taking the paragraph on p. 76 beginning, 'In the early evening . . .' and the section on p. 77 where the clock chimes, write down what sort of state you think the couple are in. Use quotations from the two passages to illustrate your answer.

Notice how Sadie's mother is still raging and worrying about her daughter (pp. 77–8). What sort of pills (pp. 69 and 71) do you think she takes?

It is typical of Kevin that he puts up a good fight when he's ambushed. Could it be partly because he's called 'traitor' again? Does this tie up with your thoughts about his reactions to the accusations of cowardice? Look back at your notes and see.

CHAPTER 10, pp. 79–87

At first sight you might be forgiven for thinking that this chapter is 100 per cent female. Then you remember that you're a careful reader, used to having second or even third thoughts about books, and you quickly cotton on to the fact that there's a very important *male* figure here too. His name is . . .? In what way does he play an important part if he isn't actually here?

Perhaps the most important and satisfying aspect of this chapter is the way that it fills out the character of Brede for us. Make a list of words which describe her.

Now think about *how* you made your list. Which of the following methods did you use?

1. Did you quite quickly *decide what you felt* about her, and then find words to describe those feelings?
2. Did you take time to *have second thoughts* and perhaps alter your first list?
3. Did you decide about Brede not only from your own feelings but also from *how others in the chapter react to her*?
4. Did you decide about Brede partly from *the way Joan Lingard describes her*?
5. Did you write your list after *reading the chapter straight through in one go*?
6. Did you read the chapter and write your list *slowly, in sections*?
7. Did you use the words which describe Brede in the book? That is, did you *use quotations*?

You will have ticked more than one of these. Whatever methods you used, it would be very surprising if you didn't use number 4.

Think again about how the author writes about Brede. Is it with:

affection
detachment
love
humour
imagination
story-telling skill
knowledge about human beings?

Now, just for interest, turn back to the 'Commentary' section and your notes on Chapter 3. You were asked what you thought about Brede then. Have you changed your mind? Learnt more about her?

This chapter is immensely serious because Brede and Sadie are. But still we get an accurately funny scene in Sadie's hat department (p. 80). Brede can't see how Sadie fits into a place like that. (Nor can Sadie, actually: see p. 7.) Obviously the saleswoman can't either, because when she announces that Sadie has been sacked, she does it 'triumphantly'. One word says a lot!

On p. 81 there's another clear little description of the sort of streets that are the setting for most of this book. They were built in the reign of Queen Victoria and are typical of Victorian industrial towns. Are there back-to-back houses where you live? Here is a plan of typical back-to-back streets:

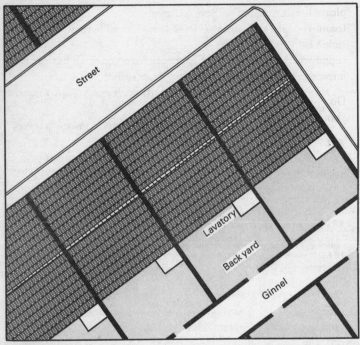

The terraced houses have small back yards, perhaps with outside lavatories in them. Each yard has a gate on to a narrow lane or ginnel; this has these back yards on both sides (hence 'back-to-back'). The streets run parallel to the ginnels outside the *front* of the terraces. The houses aren't big – probably 'two up, two down' – and the streets aren't wide; so the people living in an area like this see a lot of each other and feel they belong to a 'neighbourhood'. The corner shops and local cafés are important meeting-places.

It's not surprising, then, that Mrs McConkey and Mrs Mullet know that Brede is 'strange to the area' (p. 81).

Mrs Mullet is very funny, even if she does cause Brede's heart to thump. Her shoes play quite a part: notice where they're mentioned, and what they do in the story. Also note how the name 'Jackson' stops

Mrs Mullet in her tracks. You can almost see her mind ticking over. Write down the message it's giving her.

How would you describe Tommy here? Is he:

pleased
trusting
rude
supportive
impulsive?

Do you need help with the dialogue between Sadie and Brede at the bottom of p. 84?

SADIE: . . . It's peace at any price for him!
   (*Her idea of Tommy.*)
BREDE: Peace would be nice.
   (*Then Kevin wouldn't have to get beaten up and I wouldn't need to put myself through this frightening experience.*)
SADIE: Sometimes the price is too high.
   (*I refuse to give up Kevin just to please other people.*)
BREDE: Sometimes the price is high the other way too.
   (*You don't yet know how awful it's been for Kevin.*)

The scene in the café (*pp. 85–7*). Get together with a friend and read this scene aloud. It's practically all dialogue, and speaking it will help you to appreciate the depth of feeling of both the young women, their respect for each other, and their dignity. So much is at stake; they both love Kevin so much. The dialogue carries most of this.

Having read it aloud, write a précis of pp. 85–7. Allow yourself 150 words at the most, and try to get in *all* the feelings that Brede and Sadie go through.

Before you move on, just have another look at the last line of p. 79 and the lines 20 and 21 on p. 86. You are looking at two *similes* (comparing one thing with another, using the words 'like' or 'as if'), and very descriptive ones too. The simile (pronounced *simm*illee) is very useful if you use it sparingly and with imagination. Try one:

Getting to know a book is like . . . .

CHAPTER 11, pp. 88–95

Kevin was very badly duffed-up less than twenty-four hours ago, and getting to his meeting-point with Sadie is costing him a lot. But he still has whatever it takes to worry not only about himself on sick pay but also about what that will make his mother feel. He has also refused to let himself put a burden of danger on Brede. (Little does he know what she's done.) And he's kept his sense of humour and can grin about his 'old man's' progress. Write down what you think of him as we see him on p. 88. Also, what do you think his feelings about Sadie are? The same as hers about him? Use evidence from past chapters in what you write.

On p. 89, in the longest paragraph, it says: 'He had sent out Gerald . . . to see what Rafferty was up to . . .' Who is Gerald? Why was he a good person to choose for this job? (Have a go at finding the cross-reference for yourself. But if you're stuck, help lies at the bottom of this page.)*

Read the rest of this chapter again, paying special attention to Mr Blake. Then write a portrait of him: his appearance, if that seems important, and the kind of person he is. Don't miss his relationship with Jack; the way humans interact with their animals says a lot about them. And don't miss his attitude to Kevin and Sadie as a couple. Give your reasons for what you write.

Was doing this anything like writing about Brede in Chapter 10? Did you see any of the *same* methods? Tick YES or NO. Did you use any *different* methods? Tick YES or NO.

Religion

At the bottom of p. 91 Kevin recognizes Mr Blake as a Protestant and, over the page, is very straight with him about his own religion. That's good. But . . . how do you think Kevin *can* know Mr Blake's religion, 'at a distance of fifty yards' if necessary? Can *you* tell so quickly what a person's religion is? Can *everyone* in Northern Ireland?

* (For the really desperate!) Try Chapter 3.

What can you do to find out more about this? (If Kevin is telling the truth, doesn't it say something remarkable about the importance of religious labels?)

Sadie does two things in this chapter. (1) She meets Kevin by the river. (2) She says it's the last time she will see him. She was over half an hour late getting to Kevin, and this is the link between her actions. She left the café with twenty minutes to spare (p. 87). She had plenty of time to get to the river path. What was she doing in all that time, and why did it make her late? Anyone who has ever had to make agonizing decisions will easily be able to imagine how Sadie spent that time.

Two notes about writing. There's a marvellous example of the use of *short sentences* on p. 91: the paragraph beginning, 'She was not going to come.'* Do you see how the writing expresses Kevin's anxiety? (See the Commentary for Chapter 7, last paragraph.) And there's a surprising simile near the bottom of that page: 'legs like candles'. What do you think of that one?

CHAPTER 12, pp. 96–104

Kevin and Sadie. Poor Sadie is all set to finish their relationship, for purely unselfish reasons. She is falling in love (or has fallen – which do you think?) so it is terrible for her. What is Kevin feeling about it? Use pp. 94 and 95 in Chapter 11, plus pp. 96 and 97, and underline any of these sentences which you think are right:

- He is falling in love.
- He has fallen in love.
- He is very fond of Sadie.
- He's afraid to lose Sadie.
- He feels too ill to think much.
- He means more to her than she does to him.
- She means more to him than he does to her.

* Short *sentences*, did we say? But surely 'Safe boys.' isn't a proper sentence? No, it isn't – but good writers sometimes break rules very successfully.

Do you want to write other sentences?

Sadie blushes twice! That's surprising in someone who isn't easily embarrassed. Could it be that she finds compliments hard to accept? Mr Blake says two very nice things – about the relationship between her and Kevin, and that she's brave. Look back to the Commentary on Chapter 1, and pp. 7 and 9 in the book. Did you think that Sadie could accept compliments there? Or did she turn them into jokes, to make them easier to accept? Perhaps the person who gives the compliment makes a difference: Kevin is her age and a friend, Mr Blake is elderly and a teacher – and he's the one with the power to make her blush. What is your experience? Are there some people who can make you blush when they're nice to you?

On p. 99, line 4, Tommy asks Sadie where this business of her connection with Kevin will end. Sadie's response is revealing: she can't think about *ends*; 'Beginnings were more interesting.' She loves the excitement of new things. If she goes on feeling like that, she will have difficulty in succeeding at long-term things like further education, marriage, career and motherhood. She may make mistakes with things like managing her budget, choosing her house, or even taking up hobbies. Her brother Tommy is obviously better than she is at thinking ahead – to how things may end up. Would you say any other people in the book were 'beginners' or 'enders'? Tick the list below.

	'Beginner'	*'Ender'*
Sadie		
Tommy		
Brede		
Linda		
Mrs Mullet		
Kevin		
Brian Rafferty		
Mrs Jackson		
Mrs McCoy		

Don't tick for anybody you're not sure of, or if you think this doesn't apply to them. What about you? Your family? Your friends? How many 'beginners' and 'enders' do you know, and which do you prefer? (Is this because they're *like* you or *different* from you?)

Before you stop thinking about Sadie as a 'beginner', look at the last line on p. 100. Mrs McConkey's shop has gone, and with it a part of Sadie's childhood. What will that mean to the 'beginner' in Sadie? Refer also to p. 104, then underline any of the following possibilities:

● She will go on enjoying other parts of her childhood.
● She will find another shop where she can buy sweets and comics.
● She will start growing up.
● She will feel a gap in her life which she can't fill.
● Any other possibilities?

Mrs McConkey's shop. Read the second half of p. 99. Do you think that the incident is well described? Is it dramatic? Give reasons for your answer. If you say 'No', can you rewrite it in a more dramatic way? (If you do this, count the number of words you use and the number Joan Lingard has used. Whether you rewrite or not, notice the *kind of words* used: a lot of verbs and nouns, and remarkably few adverbs, adjectives and similes.)

Tea in the Jacksons' house (pp. 100–101). Notice Mrs Jackson's surprise at Sadie's offer to make a pot of tea; the description of the kitchen; and the comment Sadie makes about the floor. They all say something about life in the Jackson household.

Mrs Mullet and her daughter are at it again on p. 101 – making trouble. How are they doing it? A violent event seems to make a lot of people act the same way: see line 3 on p. 100.

Tommy's role here should remind you of another scene: Chapter 10, p. 83. In each case Tommy says very little, but his attitude is perfectly plain: he is *for* peace, his sister and Brede – and *against* Mrs Mullet!

The next morning (p. 102). Use your memory or the 'Summary' section to note when we first met *Steve*. Notice that here Sadie would rather not have to talk to him: she can probably guess the sort of things he'll say.

Why does *Linda* try to make it up with Sadie? Is it:

to satisfy her curiosity about Brede's visit?

to make more trouble?

because she wants to hang on to Tommy by being his sister's friend?

because she'd always rather have a nice relationship with anyone, not an uncomfortable one?

because she wonders what Sadie will do when she gets to the department store?

Mr Blake is becoming important to Sadie. He seems to represent a total contrast to her way of life (see the third paragraph on p. 100) and she places great trust in him. Does this fit in with lines 4–6 on p. 99? Think carefully. How can this be a 'beginning' for Sadie if she knows him already? After all, he did teach her at school. What's new?

By the way, who told 'the old bitch in the hat department' (p. 99) that Sadie was going out with a Mick? The same person is making trouble in this chapter too.

CHAPTER 13, pp. 105–12

From the way that Sadie talks and feels about Mrs McConkey's death (pp. 104–5) it seems as if the shopkeeper was the first person to die in the Troubles who meant something personal to her. She feels a mixture of sadness, loss, guilt at her childish naughtiness with Mrs McConkey and, on p. 104, sickness. What causes her nausea, do you think: fear, anger, a desire for revenge – any of these?

Considering how undomesticated Sadie is, it is quite courageous of her to take on domestic work for Mr Blake. Admittedly she badly needs a job. (Give the reasons: (a) . . . . (b) . . . .) All the same, it's work she normally hates and isn't good at. But she goes at it most willingly and has the reward of finding that it gives her 'a glow of satisfaction' (p. 110). Is this for any of these reasons:

- She makes the best of a bad job.
- She likes Mr Blake.
- She's more domesticated than she thought.
- She wants to prove her mother wrong.

By the way, do you really think that Mr Blake likes burnt mince?

The next thing that Sadie lets herself in for is looking after children – another uncharacteristic enterprise for her. Tick any of these reasons for her action which you think correct:

● She needs money.
● She likes Moira.
● She's interested in Moira's mixed marriage.
● . . . . ⎫ Read pp. 108 and 110
● . . . . ⎬ carefully and write
● . . . . ⎭ in more reasons

Mr Blake. There's no getting away from it – we have an elderly retired geography teacher playing a leading part in the story now. He doesn't seem to be a particularly complicated person; he's simply a warm, wise, good friend who's a bit lonely and who likes people of Sadie's and Kevin's generation.

Write a short essay on *the advantages and disadvantages of having an important adult character in a novel for teenagers.* These are some of the points you might think about:

● It's more exciting if adults stay on the fringe of the action and young people do all the big things.
● An adult point of view adds variety to the story.
● Readers like you can't get so involved with adult characters.
● Adults are only O K if they're funny or 'baddies'.
● They make an interesting contrast with the young characters.
● They give the author more story/plot possibilities.

Make your essay personal, but back up what you say using this book and any other novels you've read which are relevant. Try and write *as little as you can*, after working out your argument as carefully as you can.

If this seems a bit difficult, try to write a questionnaire on the subject and get all your class to fill it in; then present the results in a spoken report. Keep questions short and simple.

Is life easier if you're middle-class? Sadie thinks that it is – if a Protestant and a Catholic in Belfast want to get married, anyway. They'd better not try it in her working-class street, she says. (See the bottom of p. 108 and the top of p. 109.)

If you enjoy writing, you could try another essay. But this is the sort of subject that's worth talking about to all sorts of different people, because everyone has their own experiences and lots of us love arguing about the tricky matter of class. You could set up a debate on the subject: that might stop the arguments getting out of hand!

Shorter points. There's a saying, 'Set a thief to catch a thief.' Where on pp. 108–9 could you apply it?

Sadie almost slips up on p. 109, over Linda's tale-telling. Why is her question, 'Is that all?', a mistake? Her mother doesn't miss a trick – even a smile from Sadie (line 12, p. 111) arouses her suspicion. She is a worried woman.

Sadie says, 'You look a new man' to Kevin when he arrives at Mr Blake's on Friday evening. She is seeing him as grown-up. She herself is growing up fast (see the last line on p. 100 and remember her acceptance of the challenge of domesticity in this chapter). Both Kevin and Sadie show wisdom when, even though they are wrapped in happiness, they do not forget that they must protect Mr Blake (pp. 111–12).

Chapter 14, pp. 113–23

This is a very eventful chapter. If it was helpful to chart the meetings of characters in busy Chapter 9, then you can try a similar chart for this one.

Scene 1 (p. 113). This is a vivid description of Kevin's street, seen very much from his point of view. He's bored and prevented from doing his 'male' job, so the street seems narrow-minded and unpleasingly 'female'.

Scene 2 (pp. 113–15). What do you know about Mrs McCoy's (or any Catholic mother's) feelings about her son having a Protestant girlfriend? Write them down. And now look at Mrs McCoy's reaction to Mrs Kelly's talk about Kevin. Does she agree with it? Welcome it? Now write down some words to describe the kind of mother Mrs McCoy is. Do you like her? (Incidentally, notice her generous feeling

People involved	*Place*	*Mood/Emotions*
1. Kevin	Kevin's street	Restless/draggy
2.		
3.		
4.		
5. Kevin/Brede/Mr McCoy	McCoys' house	Irritation/warning/ trust/joviality
6.		
7.		
8.		
9.		
10. Kevin/Brian	Kevin's street	Suspicion

towards Mrs Kelly in the middle of p. 114: she thinks of her as 'a good-hearted woman'. She would do better to say the same thing about herself.)

Look on p. 113 at the paragraph beginning, 'Mrs McCoy lifted another shirt . . .'. It contains a clear expression of the *smallness of scale* of the back-to-back houses in Kevin's (and Sadie's) parts of Belfast. (See the Commentary for Chapter 10.) You can quite see why County Tyrone seems attractive.

This links with Kevin's attitude to Mr Blake's garden on p. 115. To a small-street, city-bred person like Kevin, soil is something which doesn't belong to you and doesn't mean anything to you, so you never get to touch it.

The following paragraph describes Kevin's wariness ever since his beating-up. If you were set an exercise to write a paragraph about a stray cat or a hunted animal, you would find several useful sentences here which would fit perfectly. Does fear always make us behave like wild animals? Have you any personal experience of this – or have you read anything else which would help you to answer this question?

By the way, at the end of this paragraph you should recognize one of the threads which join Kevin and Sadie together.

Scene 4 (pp. 116–17). When did we last see Kate? When you find the place, you will see that she said, 'I've never run after a boy in my life.' Round about the middle of p. 116 is a simile for Kate which rather contradicts that. In this scene Kate (a) tries to get Kevin to talk about himself. She then (b) talks about Brian Rafferty. Lastly (c), she tries to keep her relationship with Kevin going. In the next scene Brede warns Kevin (d) that Kate can cause trouble and is going around with Brian. What are the links between (a), (b), (c) and (d)? Do any of these seem right? Tick them if so.

- Brian Rafferty has told Kate to do (a), (b) and (c).
- He has told her to do (b).
- Kate is a schemer and a good actress.
- At (c), she isn't acting or pretending.
- (d) has got nothing to do with (a), (b) or (c).
- Any other possibilities?

What do you think of Kevin's rejection of Kate? Is he brutal? Honest? Foolish? Anything else?

To answer these questions *you do need to remember or look up* * *as many references to Kate as possible.*

In *Scene 5* Brede and Kevin nearly quarrel: she is hot and tired, he is hating the scene he's had with Kate. But Brede's perceptiveness and his trust of her turn the meeting into one of closeness.

What do you think of Mr McCoy's attitude to his new child in the paragraph on p. 118 which begins, 'Their father came in'? Does it sound as if he recognizes his share in the creation of the ninth little McCoy?

What is the most important thing about Sadie's conversation with her mother and Aunt May (p. 119)?

- It's boring.
- It makes her furious.
- Aunt May is rude and scornful.
- Her mother is rude and unsupportive.

Compare this scene with Mrs McCoy's defence of Kevin – and her respect for him – at the beginning of the chapter.

The next scene takes place in the café (pp. 120–22), where Sadie was hoping to see friends and recover her good humour. She has the bad luck to find Linda and Steve there. Early in the encounter, first Linda

---

* This is one reason for having chapter summaries.

and then Steve say provocative things to Sadie: find them and write them down. Now underline which of Sadie's words or actions are *most characteristic of her* and find a word to describe them.

Sadie is being:

1. She shrugs. ....
2. She eyes Linda warily. ....
3. 'I've nothing to talk to you about.' ....
4. She starts to rise. ....
5. 'You can lump it.' ....
6. 'I don't like anyone telling me what to do.'

Whichever you have underlined, you will notice that Sadie has her wits about her. She understands how Linda's mind works (see the bottom of p. 120). She has the sense to remain at least semi-polite ('Excuse me,' p. 121). She knows that having help from the café owner will only mean an extra black mark against her in Steve's mind. He will think she's cheated or been cowardly (see the bottom of p. 121).

Steve is very aggressive towards Sadie, yet he leaves the café obediently. Why do you think he does so?

● He only indulges in verbal, not physical, aggression.
● He's showing off to Linda.
● He's afraid of the café owner.
● He's a coward.
● He's prudent.
● What else?

When Uncle Albert tells the McCoys that their street is being searched, he provokes very different reactions from them.

Mr McCoy is ....
Brede is ....
Kevin is ....
In the street, the behaviour of the women is ....
The girls are ....
The soldiers are ....

If Uncle Albert is right about informers, *who gave the tip-off*?

CHAPTER 15, pp. 124–32

Not much that you could call 'nice' happens in this chapter at all, and it opens with a particularly unpleasant scene outside the Raffertys' house. There's Mrs Rafferty, who can scare both her big husband (see p. 47) and her big son (see p. 125), screaming at the soldiers – probably using much more unprintable words than 'eejits', too. And there's Brian. He knows that Kevin isn't the 'grass', but in a slimy way he implies that he is. The disgusting way he's chewing gum and the tough, honest response he gets – 'I hate your guts but I wouldn't inform on you' – both emphasize his nastiness.

Kevin can only retaliate by calling Brian a coward, which of course enrages him. Sadie thinks of Brian as a coward too (p. 85), and Kevin himself has been called it three times (pp. 51, 54 and 78). Which do you think is worse: to be called something bad or nasty when it's true or when it's untrue? Either way, it would take a super-person or a saint to stay calm when it happens.

Kevin behaves in a very steady manner when the army arrive to take him away – for example in his refusal of Uncle Albert's dramatic plan of escape. Then, when the army officer shows him the gun and starts asking questions, Kevin tries hard to remain steady, using lies and silence.

Commonsense must tell him to come clean about Brian showing the gun to him, to explain the ill-will between them, and thus to show that Brian has a motive for making Kevin look guilty. But he is influenced by something far stronger than commonsense. It is a sort of code of honour – something like what the Italian Mafia call *omertà*: *You never inform on* ANYONE *if the forces of authority are asking the questions. You are as good as dead otherwise.* At the same time, of course, the army officer knows about this code. And that is why (in the middle of p. 128) Kevin fears that the army will find him 'guilty by his silence'.

Kevin only unfreezes when the officer says that he's been seen with the gun. Now someone is *telling lies* about him. The awful responsibility for protecting his kind – even in the shape of Brian – drops away. Now he can defend himself. This he does stoutly, all night long.

During the night Kevin comes to a conclusion which fills him with foreboding, but which also gives him strength to overcome his sleeplessness. As he waits for Brian, the morning sun fortifies him. But he may also be feeling that it's the last time it will shine on an innocent Kevin.

Brede. This is an important chapter for her. Everything she does and almost every word she speaks confirm her as peaceable, clearsighted, loving and – in her quiet, secret way – active. (Brede has done good by stealth before. Her visit to the police station on Kevin's behalf echoes her visit to . . . . . in Chapter . . ., doesn't it?)

There is one moment with the army officer which shows Brede just as much caught up in the code of the Troubles as her brother is. Find it and note it here: it is on page . . ., lines . . . to . . . Does Brede's behaviour here influence your feelings about her? Do you now see her as:

> braver
> weaker
> nicer
> a liar
> more trustworthy
> any other description?

Mr McCoy. Right from our first meeting with him (p. 19), Mr McCoy has suffered from a bit of a persecution complex. This makes him pugnacious (the first two lines of p. 123), blustering (the middle of p. 125) and obstructive (pp. 127–8); and he rails and rages when he comes home from the police station (p. 131). (You may think that here he is indulging his complex rather unfairly: after all, Kevin is free; right has been done.)

Now look at another side of Mr McCoy. It parallels his wife's in Chapter 14 (on pp. . . . to . . .). He is tremendously supportive of Kevin. Taken in order, these are the things he does for him:

1. He tries to stop the soldiers from coming in.
2. He intervenes between Kevin and the army officer.
3. He . . . . (Fill this in.)
4. He worries when Kevin says he's going out.

Bearing this supportiveness in mind, look again at how Mr McCoy natters on on p. 131. He's just come home with Kevin after a long, long night. Imagine how he's feeling, and then underline any of these reasons for his outburst which you think are true:

- He is far too exhausted to think properly.
- He is still angry that Kevin was picked up.
- He has a bit of a persecution complex.
- He's proud of his part in Kevin's release.
- He's telling the truth about the Northern Ireland situation.
- Any other reasons?

Uncle Albert and Gerald. Each has his own way of trying to help and of giving back-up to Kevin. No doubt if Mrs McCoy hadn't been in hospital with her new baby she too would have been very supportive. It is this *strong family feeling* of 'we're all in this together' which is the one pleasant thing about this chapter. If Sadie had been in the same kind of trouble, do you think her family would have been behind her? Tick YES or NO, and write down your reasons.

The army

Use your memory and/or the 'Summary' to check on all the occasions in the book when army personnel appear. Except when they are busy chasing someone, they are always presented as fair, level-headed and conscientious. If you read newspapers regularly or have (or have heard) personal experience of Ulster, you may be surprised at Joan Lingard's soldiers.

If you think that her picture of the army is inaccurate or incomplete, write about it, giving reasons for what you say. Talk about it – preferably with someone who knows at least as much as you do. (Be prepared for heated argument!) Could your school find someone to come and talk about Northern Ireland with you?

Incidentally, did you spot the deliberate misquotation from a poem (on p. 125)? The soldiers 'had to keep their tempers whilst all around were losing theirs'. Do you know the Rudyard Kipling poem of which this is an echo? Find his poem called *If* and correct the quotation.

Two short notes. (1) The army search brings everyone in the *street* together – not in a particularly nice way, but nevertheless in a way which shows how strong a sense of *neighbourhood* everyone has. (See pp. 123, 125, and the top of p. 126.)

(2) There are two references to what the *houses* are like. On p. 125, seven lines up from the bottom, is another mention of their unlocked doors; and on p. 127, the soldiers 'stood there looking large in a small space'.

CHAPTER 16, pp. 133–40

Mr Blake's anonymous letter is not the first he's had, and this one is in a different handwriting. Does this give you a clue as to where the letters are coming from? Could they be from:

Mr Blake's enemies?
Sadie's enemies?
Kevin's enemies?
Any other idea? (*Think carefully.*)

The letters put Mr Blake in a difficult position (just as blackmail puts people in a dilemma). He has a choice of ways to behave. Look at the list of options below; think about the kind of person Mr Blake is; tick one or more if you think he *should* take them up. Also indicate if you'd approve of him for his action(s) and which *you* would have done.

1. Burn the letters and tell no one.
2. Tell Sadie and Kevin, and decide not to meet again.
3. Tell Sadie and Kevin, and let them help to decide what to do.
4. Find an excuse to give Sadie the sack (then Kevin also would stop coming).

5. Tell the police.
6. Try to find the writer(s).

Write 100 words or so about anonymous letters and their writers. (Include, if you like, what goes on on St Valentine's Day.)

However you've filled in the chart, Joan Lingard tell us that Mr Blake does in fact burn the letters. She's done this, it is fair to guess, for at least two good reasons. (1) She sees Mr Blake as the sort of person who would keep threats a secret, particularly if they involved other people's happiness. (2) Her story needs Mr Blake to burn the letters. (See how ruthless an author can be!)

Reactions to Kevin's violence
Kevin has had his revenge on Brian Rafferty. On p. 134, the conversation between him and Mr Blake is rather vague, in a way. Neither person seems to reach a conclusion; it is rather unsatisfactory. But so is a lot of conversation, particularly when you're talking about big issues.

Mr Blake can't bring himself to say that he thinks Kevin shouldn't have had his revenge. He just gets out his pipe and waffles. Do you think this is an accurate statement about him? Tick YES or NO. Find things Mr Blake says on p. 134 to back up your answer.

Although Brian has tried to frame him, *Kevin* seems in a total muddle about what he's done, and is in a bad state. Re-read the page, remembering what Brede heard in his voice an hour or two earlier (p. 131). Perhaps some of the lines which help us to follow him are, in order:

1. 'It was as if the devil was in me.'
2. 'I feel sick.'
3. 'I wanted to kill him.'
4. 'It seemed stupid somehow.'
5. 'He deserved it after all.'

The most difficult line to understand is, 'It's not that I care about him very much.' Way back on p. 47, Kevin thought, 'There were times now that Brian bored him . . .' He has grown away from Brian as a friend: on a personal level he means little. It is as a deceitful coward that he has importance. In a way, therefore, Kevin has beaten up a symbol, not a person. No wonder he's confused and sick.

Sadie's attitude at first is typically straightforward: fury at Kate, approval of Kevin, surprise at his distress. But Mr Blake makes her stop and think when he asks her, 'But what's the next thing? More blood?' Working on Kevin's bloody shirt makes the violence seem real to Sadie. And when she's had time to think, she does worry about exactly what has been done to Brian Rafferty. (Notice how, in the first half of p. 136, Mr Blake kindly but firmly helps her to think this through. He gives her facts, and allows her to make up her own mind about whether or not Kevin would use a weapon.)

The graffiti (*pp. 137–8*)

The word 'traitor' – like the word 'coward' – runs through the book. This is the first time it's been applied to Sadie. Who are the two people who are 'going to have a stroke' if they see the graffiti? Who do you think painted it?

Tommy is very tolerant. Having said that he wishes Sadie would stop seeing Kevin, and been given the brush-off, he shuts up about it. Actually, do you think that 'tolerant' is the right word for him? If there's another description you'd prefer, write it down now.

Mrs Jackson. Earlier in this chapter, Mr Blake thinks of Sadie as 'very sharp'. She's inherited it from her mother, who yet again (as on pp. 77–8) notices Sadie smiling and has her suspicions.

Someone else is very sharp. They are keeping an eye on their graffiti and re-painting it (p. 139).

The day out (*pp. 139–40*)

Kevin and Sadie have come to rely on Mr Blake. He is a friend and counsellor and his house is their refuge. He is obviously very happy with this, and makes the most of it (he probably hasn't had many trips out in the car since his wife died). Yet look at the age difference between him and them: more than forty years. Pretend that you know the three and that someone says, 'I don't believe you can make friends with people of a different generation.' Write a letter to this person, explaining how the threesome works so well in this case. Add any personal experiences you may have (remembering younger as well as older people in your life).

CHAPTER 17, pp. 141–50

The first page of this chapter establishes that – as you probably guessed – the car has been sabotaged and that Mr Blake's careful driving has saved their lives.

On p. 142, why do Sadie and Kevin look at one another when the plain-clothes policemen show their cards? Do you think it is because:

- They didn't realize at first that the men were police.
- They're signalling to one another that they'll keep back information.
- They are nervous.

Underline any you think true; or write down what you think the reason is.

You know, we all know, that the crash was sabotage. What possible reason can Mr Blake and Kevin have for calling it an 'accident' (p. 142)? Perhaps

- They really think it was.
- They can't bear to think it was sabotage.
- They don't want the police to know that *they know* it was sabotage.

Again, underline your choice.

A point about the writing in this scene. Whatever their reasons, all three of them have got to come to terms with the fact that someone wants one or all of them dead, and that the police are going to probe. They each sit having frightening, puzzling thoughts and saying not a word. They are separated from each other as well as from the police. Two pages later (p. 144) they are in the same situation. And each time, they are written about in the same order. By using this rather formal, stylized way of showing how Sadie, Kevin and Mr Blake are feeling, Joan Lingard emphasizes their fear and isolation. She also highlights the isolation of the police, for unless people talk to them, they cannot do their job. (See the bottom of p. 130 for the army officer's reaction to silence.)

Now turn back to p. 143. The policeman breaks the silence: 'Have you any idea who might have done this?' Sadie – typically – wakes up first. Then the policeman turns to Mr Blake, who says – 'with a little smile' – he doesn't know anyone who'd want to kill him. What does that smile mean? Could it be that Mr Blake is pleased that by being able to tell the truth (and indeed he doesn't *know* his enemy) he can take the pressure off Sadie and Kevin? He's presumably not smiling because there's anything funny going on. But there is one other possible cause for a smile – a rather wry* smile. He's led a life quite without enemies up to now, and he doesn't deserve to have any. So – can you write down a second reason for his smile?

In the second half of the interview (pp. 145–6) and for a moment in the first half (at the top of p. 143) Sadie is . . . . How would you describe her? Read her dialogue with the policeman and find three or four adjectives for her.

In your work on Chapter 16, when you were thinking about Mr Blake's options for dealing with anonymous letters, did you think that he should tell the police? Now he's done it (p. 146), do you think he's right? Right, but too late? Or wrong?

On p. 147, Mr Blake starts his conversation with Moira by saying, 'I'm glad you and Mike are happy.' Why? Tick *one* of the following:

- He likes Moira and Mike.
- He's surprised that a Catholic and Protestant can marry successfully.
- He's sad, and wants to talk about something nice.
- He's hoping Sadie and Kevin will also end up being happy together.

---

* Look this word up in a dictionary if you don't know it. You might want to use it yourself one day in the not-too-distant future.

Useful hint. Remember where, when and how Mr Blake talks about the satisfactions he gets out of his relationship with Kevin and Sadie.

Mr Blake goes indoors again and his friends tell him that they've decided not to come and see him any more. Write a version of this scene (up to line 7, p. 148) *using no dialogue* but writing down how the characters think and feel. This may help you to grasp what makes Kevin and Sadie change their minds – from not seeing Mr Blake to seeing him occasionally.

In the very next paragraph, Kevin changes his mind again. Why is decision-making so difficult for him and Sadie?

- They're bad at making decisions.
- They know they must make decisions which will be painful.
- They're in an emotional state and can't think clearly.

Mr Kelly's scrapyard (pp. 148–9)
In this scene, Kevin gets back a lot of his vigour. He hates injustice and always reacts strongly to it. (We know this because of his actions in Chapters . . . and . . .) It is a pity that he over-reacts this time: 'Mr Kelly called to him to stop but he did not.' Mr Kelly has always liked and trusted Kevin: he hates giving him the sack – he can't look him in the eye. After his first angry response to Kevin's accusations about Kate, he wants to find out more. He thinks that Kevin may be telling the truth. But Kevin blows any chances of explanation – or of keeping his job; he is too deeply angry to act sensibly.

Two points to note on pp. 149–50. (1) Brede's guess that Kevin would be sacked by Kate's father – another example of her accurate observation of the world. (2) Mr McCoy doesn't like Kevin losing his job, and makes that clear, but his first instinct is to defend his son. (When did he last do that? Jot down in which chapter he did so.)

More about the writing. On p. 150, in remarkably few words, Joan Lingard makes us see Kevin's rejection, anxiety, depression, restlessness and sadness, and also his strong will-power. If you, or someone you know, or a character you invent, have been through a really bad patch – or a really good one – can you describe it? (From 'It did not take long . . .' to the end of the page, Joan Lingard spends 226 words. You may have up to 326, as she's had more practice.)

CHAPTER 18, pp. 151–61

Violence

As the Twelfth of July approaches, so the violence builds up to its annual climax. The army is expecting trouble and has been reinforced.

If you, the reader, are expecting or even hoping for big trouble and a climax of blood, noise and action, you must give up that thought at once. Joan Lingard doesn't write novels in that macho way. Nor is she writing a documentary. *The Troubles are the foundation of her story, not the subject.* Her main characters are influenced and affected by the political/religious passions in Northern Ireland and are drawn into them very reluctantly. If Brian Rafferty and Steve were the main characters, that would be a different kettle of fish (and the book might need a different author).

On p. 151, Mrs Jackson says, 'It's not safe to be out in the evenings nowadays.' Sadie hears the peaceful (though, to Catholics, provocative) sounds of band and drum practice. Later in the week Kevin in his Catholic quarter sees the aftermath of rioting and looting and is revolted.

For a moment we'll look ahead to pp. 158–9. This extended descriptive passage (rare for Joan Lingard) is very effective. Pick out for yourself the words, phrases and sentences which you find most expressive. (You are looking at 'Kevin came out of the supermarket . . .' (p. 158) to 'Yelling for blood' (p. 159).)

Children and violence

The children Sadie hears on p. 151 and the ones Kevin sees on p. 159 seem different. There could be several reasons for this:

- Protestant children are nicer than Catholic ones.

- All kids get more violent as the 'Twelfth' draws nearer.
- Catholic children have more grievances than Protestant ones.
- Sadie's worried sadness and Kevin's intense loathing make them each perceive the children differently.
- Sadie *hears* the kids in her street; Kevin *sees* them in his.
- Any other points?

Do some cross-referencing: Where in the book have Gerald and other children played an active part?

If you've read *The Twelfth Day of July* you'll know what Kevin and Sadie were like as young teenagers. But can you imagine how they'd have behaved when they were, say, eight or nine? Think what their parents and siblings * are like, as well as themselves, and write a short description of each of them as little kids.

Taking the rest of the chapter in order. On p. 152, on the 'Twelfth', we get echoes of Chapter 2: that's where we first heard of Mr Jackson's Lodge and his wife's rollers. You can tell how important this day is to her, because she takes them out in the *morning*!

At the top of p. 153, Tommy goes out to watch the parade, *avoiding Sadie's eye*. Why? Is he slightly ashamed of showing interest in Orange business? Does he wonder what Sadie's going to get up to? Probably a bit of both.

In Bangor (pp. 153–5)
You know the saying, 'Absence makes the heart grow fonder'. Well, it seems to be true. Kevin and Sadie are very tender and affectionate: he in particular seems to have grown fonder. Pick out things he says or does which show his love for Sadie.

On p. 154, nine lines up from the bottom, Sadie thinks, 'Some of his gaiety had gone. He was changing.' The event which started Kevin's change was . . . . In Chapter 14, there is evidence of his change on pages . . . . In this chapter there are . . . occasions when he says he'll leave Belfast. And on pp. 160–61 his hatred of the political situation is growing almost uncontrollably. Can you find or remember other examples of Kevin losing his gaiety? Note them down (for example the one on p. 156).

* Did you look this up when you were working on Chapter 4?

Notice how Sadie's and Kevin's resolution not to meet fades away in Bangor, and how they arrange to go back to using Mr Blake's house as a refuge. That may be the power of love – but is it wise? Think what you would have done in their situation and write it down. Is it similar to what these two did?

Mr and Mrs McCoy's departure (*pp. 155–7*)

This scene is a pleasant relief from violence and sadness, and it's nice to welcome back funny old Uncle Albert and his amazing car. Kevin is feeling better because he's seeing Sadie. Compare the last paragraph on p. 157 with the description of the streets on pp. 158–9: how happy and beautiful life can be. In your opinion, is Joan Lingard as good at describing happiness as violence?

Before you leave p. 157, look at the first paragraph. What opinion have you about Kevin's father's attitude to domestic work? What does he call it? '. . . . .' What do you think Kevin's thoughts are about being left in charge of the house? And, by the way, why has the job fallen on him? Because (1) . . . . and (2) . . . .

It's nice that on p. 158 Kevin pays tribute to his sister. And it's good, too, to have a bit of comedy from Sadie. What put the idea for her excuse to the butcher into her mind?

Mr Kelly's scrapyard (*pp. 159–60*)

Poor Mr Kelly. He's a decent man who likes Kevin and values him. He's a brave man, too: he has the courage to ask for forgiveness and to express his need. (Have you ever tried either of those? It's not easy!) But Mr Kelly is defeated by the change in Kevin and his polite firmness. It is rather sad.

Mrs Rafferty is, as usual, unpleasant. She cannot resist making life nasty for Kevin. ('Getting the messages' means 'doing the shopping' – women's work.)

She is the last straw that day. Kevin may think that he can 'stand the cracks', but he is in fact near to cracking – or bursting. Joan Lingard finds a graphic and disgusting simile (pp. 160–61) to express Kevin's disgust. (There is another boil near the end of Chapter 10.

Find it and decide which you think makes the better simile. Or are they both good?)

Summary
These ten pages are full of a great variety of *moods*. It might help you to keep them all in your mind if you listed the moods in order, and the characters involved. It would be an efficient way to summarize the chapter.

Chapter 19, pp. 162–8

It is ironic that the Jacksons talk about 'getting used to the murders' as they sit in the small hours drinking tea with the guns going off outside. For as soon as a murder actually touches their lives they all, not only Sadie, feel a lot – particularly Mrs Jackson, which might surprise you. Up to now she's seemed not all that nice, and not very nice to Sadie. But when she hears that Mr Blake has been killed (p. 164) she puts her hand to her throat, a very common gesture of distress and fear. She has a heart, after all.

The night before (three lines up from the bottom of p. 162), Mrs Jackson has been as sharp as ever, spotting Sadie's smile as she thinks about Kevin. How does Sadie know that he'll wait for her if she's late? He's done it before, hasn't he?

Mike Henderson brings the news
On the last line of p. 163 and the first of p. 164, Sadie 'felt that she had lived through this moment before'. So she has – but last time the grief and the guilt were not as strong; it was when Brede told her about Kevin's beating-up (p. 85).

Her feeling of guilt over Mr Blake's death almost overcomes her instinct for survival; on p. 164 she very nearly blurts out that she's been seeing Kevin in Mr Blake's house all this time. (She's been keeping all her meetings with him secret for ages – ever since Chapter

9.) Mike Henderson saves her now, first by trying to stop her talking, second by fobbing off Mr Jackson. He's also very helpful about getting Sadie to her meeting with Kevin (pp. 165–6). Why should he be so quick to help?

● He's a nice man.
● He likes Sadie and Kevin.
● He too is in a mixed-religion relationship.
● He does it in memory of Mr Blake.

If you ticked all of those, all your ticks would be right. Do you agree?

Poor Mike: his kindness to Sadie means that he has to break the awful news to a second person (p. 166). Mr and Mrs Jackson think that Mike is taking Sadie back to his house, thanks to his quickness in preventing Sadie from giving her secret away. Do you think that Tommy guesses what she's really going to do?

The writing of this scene. From Mike's car arriving (p. 163) to the time he and Sadie leave her house (top of p. 166), nearly everything is written in dialogue. The characters speak in short sentences. Most of the action is written in short sentences. We've looked before at how mood and pace and atmosphere can be created with short, clipped writing (see pp. 59 and 91, for instance) and at how well Joan Lingard's dialogue carries the story along (she is a playwright as well as a novelist, after all). Do you know people who are good at emotional acting? This scene would be very strong as drama.

The funeral and after (pp. 166–8)
Sadie's condition over the days between Mr Blake's death and his funeral is written about in a very different way. Read from 'It was a big funeral . . .' to '. . . to think at once of Mr Blake.'

● Is there much dialogue?
● Is it written with urgency?
● Is it written with intensity?
● What is the main difference in writing technique between p. 163 to the top of p. 166 and this passage?

You may wonder why Moira and Sadie don't go to Mr Blake's

funeral (p. 166). It's because, quite commonly in Northern Ireland, women don't go to funerals – not even if the dead person was one of their closest relatives.

Five lines up from the bottom of p. 166, Sadie says, 'It doesn't seem possible.' Yet on the morning she was told about the bomb and the death she expresses, first, disbelief and then *she begins to accept the truth*: 'The knowledge was seeping through to her brain.' Using your knowledge of her feelings over these few days (and personal experience, if you can), write a paragraph explaining why Sadie moves between rejection and acceptance of this awful event.

Moira and Mike have almost had a row (p. 167). On the face of it, it was about sending their children away to Moira's mother. Is this the only reason? There could be others:

- Mike might dislike Moira's mother.
- He and Moira might feel that they were being cowardly.
- Moira might be feeling angry with herself for getting involved with Sadie and Kevin.
- Both the Hendersons might be very upset and be taking it out on each other.
- Any other reasons?

When Mike and Kevin come in from the funeral (notice that the women aren't offered whisky) Kevin flares up with anger and a desire for revenge. Mike had a flash of anger in Sadie's house. Did *he* want revenge? He talks Kevin into calmness (at the top of p. 168). But in the end Kevin would probably have decided for himself against revenge of any kind: he's tried it once and found it a very confusing and distressing business. Find the place where this happened and re-read it.

On Cave Hill (p. 168)

Kevin's speech to Sadie here is short, although it's so important. This is because he and she know and trust one another so completely. Partly as a writing exercise, partly to make sure you absolutely understand how Kevin's mind works, re-write his speech. Pretend that he's explaining himself to his parents. You will have to write more than he says to Sadie, but you have plenty of material to draw on, even if you only use Kevin's thoughts over the last two chapters. Remember, *Kevin is not a coward* and he wants to make sure his parents realize that.

What are Sadie's feelings as she sees Belfast Lough 'blur and then come sharply into focus again'? (Is the word 'sharply' a hint?) Write them down.

CHAPTER 20, pp. 169–74

Do you think that this farewell scene (up to p. 172) is moving or touching? If you do, it is worth pointing out that it is one of the longest and most detailed scenes in the whole book. What's more, if you read it aloud it would take up just about the same amount of time as actors would need to perform it.* The scene is fully written, but not over-written. It is long enough for sadness, but not long enough for sentimentality. By writing so truthfully and warmly about the McCoys, it's as if Joan Lingard has given them all a farewell hug.

Details. Why do Brede and Kevin make little jokes? Why does Mr McCoy take it for granted that Kevin's going to live in Liverpool? When did we last see Mrs McCoy make a careful fuss over a meal for a journey? Why does Mr McCoy clear his throat?

And why, do you think, does Kevin want to go alone to the docks for his ship? Is it because:

- He doesn't want any fuss?
- He feels he doesn't deserve a proper send-off?
- He doesn't want to be seen feeling sad or nervous?
- He's pretty sure that Sadie will be there to see him off?

Which, if any, of these have you ticked?

On p. 171 Mr McCoy gives Kevin a fiver. That wouldn't go far today, but in 1972, when this book was published, it was worth a great deal more, and would be a big slice out of Mr McCoy's wage packet.

*See also, for example, p. 12 (second half) to p. 16 (first half), and p. 49 (second half) to p. 50.

Notice Brede's part in this scene. She's *supportive* (for instance when she frees Kevin from having to reply to the unspeakable Mrs Rafferty on p. 172). She's *unobtrusive*, and perfectly prepared to accept that Kevin wants to leave alone. And she's *picked out* by him as the one person he will go down the street with.

If you've ever had to say goodbye and leave someone for a long time, which was the worst part? Was it:

- When you saw what the time was?
- When you kissed goodbye?
- When the door closed behind you?
- When the house went out of sight?
- Any other awful moment?

Kate Kelly

Is she apologizing to Kevin on p. 173? Or just trying to excuse herself? Compare her encounter with Kevin with her father's on pp. 159–60. Which of the Kellys do you respect more?

For once, Kate does Kevin a good turn. Her 'Brian Rafferty made me' is important: 'Made you?' he repeats. That 'made' stands for force, violence, unwilling behaviour, a bad way of living – and he suddenly realizes that it no longer need mean anything to him at all.

Sadie

There can be no doubt that both she and Kevin knew all along that she would be at the dockside. And we can't be surprised that she's decided to go with him, knowing her flamboyant spirit. But not being surprised mustn't prevent you from appreciating her courage. She's kept her big secret from her unhelpful parents to the end, and is launching into the blue with nothing but her ticket and what she stands up in.

*

Joan Lingard was asked: *What do you think about people reading* Across the Barricades *because they've been told to, rather than because they want to?*

'My attitude to my books is that I write them and then it's like casting your bread upon the water, and you can't do anything about it.

'Of course I would rather have people read them because they want to. That was why I was very pleased with the "Teen Read" thing, where a teenage jury chose their top twenty books from a shortlist of 100. *Across the Barricades* was one of them. I was pleased about that because it was chosen by young people themselves, not by teachers or librarians or whatever.'

Would *you* put *Across the Barricades* in your Top Twenty? There are five Kevin and Sadie novels altogether. So if you've had not only hard work but also fun and pleasure with this one, a feast awaits you!

Characters

'My characters are shaped by the environment they have been born into,' says Joan Lingard. 'The children of Northern Ireland are different from other children because of their political and religious inheritance.' In the Kevin and Sadie books, all the young people 'live very close to one another, and they all come from similar backgrounds: working-class families who don't think very deeply about anything, but adhere to the general view'.

But they change; some of them become mature at an early age. 'I think that when they start off they're not all that mature. At the end of *The Twelfth Day of July* they change because of the trouble that happens on the night of the eleventh, when Brede nearly dies from an injury. They change through this next book because as characters they have the possibility of change within them, and the intelligence to look out and to say, "This isn't all – we don't want to live with this violence." They mature with that.

'I think they are very streetwise; they're urban kids, they know what's what. They're not sheltered, they're not protected, they're not in neat little parcels, they're not dressed up. They know what the score is, and don't duck it.

'I like streetwise kids. They give me something to write about.'

SADIE AND KEVIN

These two are of course the most important characters in the book – its 'heroine' and 'hero' – but it is important to see them as two distinct people, not two look-alikes. Important, but not always easy, because one of the strongest threads which tie them together is in fact *their similarity of attitude* to things. So let's look at this first and clear the difficulty out of the way.

There are references to their shared attitudes on pp. 6, 10, 28, 55, 76 and 116. Make a list of them. Now write down the reason(s) why these similarities draw Kevin and Sadie close to one another.

If you think there are other characteristics that the couple share, write these down too. Now we are in the clear and can look at them individually.

Sadie

If you actually met Sadie Jackson you might find her a bit tiring, because she has a huge amount of *physical and mental energy*; she is seldom still or silent. Imagine you told her straight out that she was exhausting you; how do you think she would react? Tick any of these that seem likely:

with anger
with amazement
with apologies
with a joke about your feebleness
with a joke about her restlessness
in some other way.

There is one place in the book (pp. 151–2) where Sadie spends a lot of time just sitting in her bedroom. This is so unusual that her mother asks her, 'Are you sickening for something?' But even here, though Sadie's body is still, her energetic mind is still whirling.

Sadie puts energy into her responses to things, too. For instance, on p. 41 she makes her mother catch her breath with the defiance she throws at Mr Jackson when he tries to control her. On pp. 53–4 she's first into the freezing swimming pool in Bangor. On p. 102 she explodes at Mrs Mullet and Linda's insinuation that Brede caused Mrs McConkey's shop fire. On p. 106 as soon as she gets her job with Mr Blake she is 'gripped by a fever for action'. And so on: you will easily pick out more examples.

If you had to describe Sadie's energetic response to life in one word, which of these would you pick?

    exaggerated
    manic
    generous
    warm-hearted

Now add another word of your own. . . . .

Sadie and Kevin have two quarrels, on pp. 31 and 56–7. Each is about Kevin's religion, and Sadie starts them both. This is not because she is quarrelsome. She really has a blind spot about Catholicism, which she hates (and perhaps fears?). This is an example of someone who, Joan Lingard says, 'doesn't think very deeply, but adheres to the general view'. (In Sadie's case, the general *Protestant* view.) It is quite hard to understand and accept this from such an open, intelligent person, and to reconcile it with her love for a Catholic boy. If you learn about the religious divide in Northern Ireland, it will help. So might discussion and argument. Do you known of any relationships which mix religious faiths? Do the couple quarrel about it? Religion and politics are both famous for being impossible to argue about politely.

Is Sadie a liar? Yes, she is. In order to go on seeing Kevin she lies to her parents from Chapter 10 right up to the last page of the book. But does she lie to anyone else – or about anything else? No, she does not. Circumstances and her emotions turn her into a limited liar. Kevin says to her on p. 7, 'You never found it easy to tell a lie, did you?' So, in a perverse way, her lying takes courage and appears not wrong but absolutely right. Bearing all this in mind, write the letter Sadie must have written to her parents when she and Kevin got to England. Can you get in some Sadie-type humour as well? (Perhaps about her lack of luggage, or her fellow passengers on the boat, or English accents.)

Kevin

The size of the McCoy family has a big influence on Kevin. He is the oldest of eight children when the books starts; his wage as a working man is important to the household; his authority will be useful in a crowded house. These responsibilities have matured Kevin. (Can you imagine him being as impetuous and wild as Sadie is?) And the events in the book change him further.

He has a passionate temper, and he's physically strong. (See him at work pp. 47–9, and fronting up to Brian on p. 50 and Mr Mullet on pp. 70–71.) He puts both these aspects of himself to use in his revenge on Brian. Yet even as he does so, he wonders what he is doing, and why; and when he tells Mr Blake about it (p. 134) he feels sick. His own almost murderous violence – which he committed quite deliberately – confirms another side of him, his hatred of violence.

Before we leave the subject of Kevin and violence, you must be sure that you understand why he beats up Brian. It is not because Brian & Co. beat *him* up. It's because...................................
And the reason is that the way the Troubles corrupt people's morals really gets to Kevin.

Considering what a rough, tough life Kevin lives, and his restless, adventurous nature, it is remarkable how soft and tender he can be with Sadie. He doesn't seem to have any male models of a softer kind he can copy: his father, Uncle Albert, Mr Rafferty and Mr Kelly all leave something to be desired as husbands. It says a lot for Kevin's inner security and faith in himself that he can let his loving feelings show. (Though you may think that he is slower to fall in love with Sadie than she is with him. And one day he'll have to learn to cope with women when they cry – see p. 117.)

Perhaps it is his mixture of 'tough and tender' which makes Kevin attractive to girls. If you are a girl, write a description of Kevin as if you rather fancied him. If you are a boy, write a description of Kevin as if your girlfriend rather fancied him. (You will find physical descriptions of Kevin on pp. 5, 27, 50 and 154.)

Will Kevin make a good husband? Write down reasons for your answer.

There is another thing about Kevin which must be very important to Sadie: he trusts her absolutely. He knows that, whatever the difficulties, she will always meet him as they have arranged (for example on the day after his beating-up – p. 92). He knows that she'll be at the dockside to see him off (p. 173). He even seems to know that he'll see her in Bangor again (p. 153). Kevin is good at trusting. There are two other characters he puts total faith in. They are ....
and ....

THE JACKSON FAMILY

Perhaps Sadie is such an independent person because there isn't much closeness between herself and Mr and Mrs Jackson. Her mother is sharply critical of her (for instance on pp. 12 and 101–2) and her father seems interested in her only because she's mixed up with a Catholic. Mrs Jackson is a good housewife, but she takes pills. Do you imagine her as:

fat	brisk
thin	smiling
slow–moving	frowning?

Mr Jackson has a strong commitment to the Orange Order, so Kevin's connection with his daughter seems intolerable to him. When he, Mr Mullet and Tommy meet Sadie and Kevin coming home from Bangor in the small hours (pp. 69–70), Mr Jackson thinks it more important to fight Kevin than to know that his daughter is safe.

Using the 'Summary' section, look up the scenes between Sadie and either or both of her parents and make up your mind whether or not she loves them or they her, and, if so, how much. You will need to 'read between the lines', as they say.

Tommy

Tommy is a year older than Sadie and a good deal steadier – and duller. He's a nice, thoughtful young man and has a steady job in the shipyards. It is sad for him that he hasn't Sadie's daring spirit, because it means that he will never re-create his feelings for Brede (p. 17). He does a lot for Sadie:

- He tries to stop Linda telling his parents about Sadie seeing Kevin again (p. 14).
- He tells Sadie not to see Kevin any more (p. 42).
- He prevents Mr Jackson from fighting Kevin (p. 70).

- He prevents a really big fight from happening (pp. 71–2).
- He gets Mrs Mullet out of the way so that Brede can see Sadie (pp. 83–4).
- He tries to get rid of the 'traitor' graffiti on their house (p. 137).
- He tells Sadie she should stop seeing Kevin for her own good (p. 138).

Most of these are rather negative. Is that because Tommy is a negative sort of person, or that he can't see ahead very positively? Do you think that he tried to help in the right ways? Tick the ones you approve of.

Pretend that Tommy is applying for a better job in the shipyards and write a personal reference for him.

THE McCOY FAMILY

The four oldest people in the McCoy household – the parents, Kevin and Brede – have far stronger links of affection than most of the Jacksons have.

Mr McCoy

Mr McCoy is the least demonstrative, but he certainly does his bit for Kevin when the soldiers take him off to the police station (p. 129). Do you think that it's funny when Mr McCoy rages about the political situation (particularly on p. 131)? Tick YES or NO. If you ticked YES, is that because:

- Mr McCoy's just a silly old bletherer.
- He's not the sort of man to turn from words to violence.
- He's powerless to do anything about the situation, however much he goes on about it.

A tick for any of these could make sense. But you should realize that he is actually expressing deep-rooted ideas, feelings, prejudices – whatever you want to call them. His raging is as serious to him as Sadie's anger about the Pope is to her, and as difficult to change.

Mrs McCoy

On the face of it, you'd think that *she* should be taking the pills, not Mrs Jackson. She has a house overflowing with children, several of them rather wild, particularly Gerald – and none too much money. For a lot of the book she is pregnant. And she doesn't like living in Belfast; Tyrone is where she'd rather be. How does she manage?

- Her religion helps her.
- She's used to her life and runs it well.
- She's used to being pregnant.
- She's the sort who wouldn't feel alive unless they were worrying.
- Brede helps her a lot.
- Kevin is reliable and helpful.
- She doesn't manage all that well – she's tired and old before her time.

Tick any of these which seem right.

Brede

Brede is the McCoys' eldest daughter, one year younger than Kevin. He is lucky in his sister. She's very fond of him indeed, as you can tell from their 'goodbye' scene on p. 172. And she has a sort of genius for *putting her love for others to work*. She does this literally: her waged job is with children, her unwaged job is helping her mother with house-work and childcare. And Brede has the gift of perception (what is sometimes – and sometimes scathingly – called 'feminine intuition'):

- She spots the start of Kate and Brian's relationship (p. 76) and sees it develop (p. 118).

- She knows that Kevin's going on seeing Sadie and that he's keen on her (p. 118).
- She names Kate as the 'witness' to Kevin's supposed gun-running (p. 129). (Mr McCoy is proud of her at this moment: 'She's got a fine instinct. Just like her mother,' he says.)
- She realizes that Kevin's going to have his revenge on Brian (pp. 131–2).

This list is incomplete; you could find more examples of Brede's understanding. Note how it is far more positive than Tommy's rather negative list. And don't forget that Brede is more than just a quiet, sensitive person. She twice, at crucial moments in the story, is both physically active and very brave (see Chapters 10 and 15). She also has the moral courage to speak out against violence and bloodshed (for example on pp. 75 and 87).

What kind of work would you like Brede to get when she leaves home? Do you think any of these jobs would suit her?

policewoman	probation officer
air hostess	priest
personnel officer	prime minister
doctor	psychiatrist
teacher	What else?
wife and mother	

Uncle Albert

Uncle Albert is a sponger (p. 20) and not a particularly considerate husband (pp. 62 and 67). He's a bit feckless – he can't be bothered to look after his car properly (p. 64). And he gets wild, impetuous ideas, like rescuing Kevin from the police (p. 127). But he's a cheerful soul and happy to drive his family about in his dreadful car; he takes Mr and Mrs McCoy to Tyrone, for instance (p. 156). He's also:

extrovert
funny

non-political
What else?

Do you like Uncle Albert? Write down reasons for your answer.

THE MULLETS

The Mullets are a Protestant family in Sadie's street.

Mrs Mullet

It is often hard to dislike Mrs Mullet, because she is funny. But make a list of the things she does, and they will look like the actions of a horrible person.

Find a word or phrase for this

She's a scandalmonger with 'the longest tongue in the street' (p. 33).
She's a scrounger (p. 34).
She eavesdrops on Mrs Jackson being rude about her (p. 36).
In revenge, she spreads gossip about Sadie 'walking out with a Mick' (pp. 36–7).
She tries to find out who Brede is (pp. 82–4).
She implies that Brede burned down Mrs McConkey's shop (p. 101).

Mr Mullet

Mr Mullet isn't nearly as powerful as his wife: for instance, when Mrs McConkey's shop is in flames all he does is stand waving his arms. His big scene is at the beginning of Chapter 9. He is rather wimpish on p. 68, then clumsily insulting to Sadie, annoying her father (p. 69). He provokes Kevin to violence (p. 70), then wants to back out of the whole thing (p. 71) and goes home as fast as he can (p. 72).

Linda

Linda Mullet is a chip off her mother's block. She too loves scandal and spreads it as easily as you'd spread margarine. Being younger and perhaps cleverer than her mother, Linda also uses her charms (lowering her eyelashes, showing off her legs – see p. 13) to tantalize her victims. She's keen to keep Tommy in her clutches, so her charms come in useful with him too. (He thinks that she can be 'very soft and sweet' – p. 38.)

Make a list of Linda's actions, like the one for her mother, and find words to describe them. You need to look at pp. 8–9, 13–18, 37–41, 100–103 and 120–21. Do you think that Linda is nastier or less nasty than her mother? Do you think she got Sadie the sack from the hat department? Tick YES or NO to the last question. Do you think Tommy is a bit slow to ditch her (on p. 40)? Tick YES or NO.

THE RAFFERTYS

The Raffertys are a Catholic family in Kevin's street. Mr Rafferty has fathered a son who is very like him both in body and mind. He himself drinks a lot. He is frightened of his screeching wife, who is able to control her son as well as her husband (p. 125). Mrs Rafferty makes her mark on the street by shouting and screaming in a loud and unpleasant voice. She deserves to be married to a bully and to be the mother of a bullying son. The Rafferty household (on the few occasions when all three are in) must be very unattractive.

Brian

Brian Rafferty belongs to the Provisional I R A and subscribes to the idea that violence gets things going your way. He is the character in this book who sticks most closely to an idea without thinking deeply about it. It is this lack of development in him that first puts Kevin off him: they used to be friends, but Kevin grows away from him.

One can foresee a sticky end for Brian because he will spend his life fighting dirty. He is a great one for shouting 'Coward!' at people: yet *he* is cowardly in the way he gets Kevin beaten up – and even more so if it was he who organized the killing of Mr Blake. In this way he is like people who are against sexual behaviour in others because their own sex lives are difficult.

STEVE

Steve is a Protestant who was at school with Tommy Jackson. He was rather keen on Sadie.

He too may be a coward, for he was probably the one who sent some of the anonymous letters to Mr Blake, and he may in fact have killed him. Steve joins the Orange Lodge (p. 38), but not for the same reason that Mr Jackson has for being a member. Sadie's father belongs because it 'reaffirms his (Protestant) faith' (p. 12). It looks as if Steve may have joined in order to hype himself up for political action, which will include violence. (On p. 102, after Mrs McConkey's shop has been set alight by the Catholics, Steve takes it for granted that people like him will take reprisals.)

On that occasion, Sadie snubs Steve: she thinks very little of him. Then, a couple of weeks later, she has a verbal and psychological battle with him in the café (pp. 120–21). Steve has the worst of it, partly because he himself is weak. But he feels 'murderous'. *If* he sent Mr Blake the letters, *if* he tampered with his car or bombed his house, Sadie was foolish to treat Steve with such contempt.

Do you think that he had the personal or political motive to do, or attempt to do, murderous things? You need to be a coward with big ideas to perform such high cowardly actions. Is Steve big enough? Remember an important piece of evidence on p. 133: the anonymous letters were not all written in the same handwriting. Write a report on Steve as if you were a member of the police force trying to solve the mystery of Mr Blake's death.

THE KELLYS

This Catholic family lives round the corner from Kevin's street in a house next to Mr Kelly's scrapyard. Because they only have three children – two off their hands – and because the scrapyard is successful, the Kellys are better off than the other households in the area. Kevin works for Mr Kelly and Kate considered Kevin to be her boyfriend.

Mrs Kelly

Mrs Kelly has only a small part to play in the book. Perhaps her role in life in general is pretty small? In Chapter 14, when she's visiting Mrs McCoy, and McCoy baby no. 9 indicates that it's on the way, Mrs Kelly gets flustered. Mrs McCoy doesn't think much of her ironing, either.

Mrs Kelly has come to talk to Mrs McCoy about Kevin (who has been beaten up) and his Protestant girlfriend. She isn't prying with any evil intent. Her reaction to the trouble Kevin is creating is like her reaction to Mrs McCoy's request for an ambulance. Which of these words fit Mrs Kelly's attitude?

worried	silly
hesitant	nervous
peace-loving	undomesticated
incompetent	muddled

Tick as many as you think accurate. Add more if you want to.

Mr Kelly

Mr Kelly's work with scrap has made him a strong little man. He organizes his life quite well: he works hard but not too hard; he doesn't rush; and he takes a full hour for lunch (p. 49). He's not over-generous with his payment of Kevin, but he likes him and shows it. (For instance, look at his friendly behaviour to Kevin on p. 49.)

This liking makes it hard for Mr Kelly to sack Kevin (pp. 148–9). He only has Kate's word for it that Kevin hid the gun in the scrapyard: the chances are that if Kevin hadn't called Kate a liar, the two men could have talked things through and no sacking would have occurred. Mr Kelly would rather trust a man than a woman; but he also has old-fashioned ideas about women needing protection, so the insulter of his daughter has to go.

On pp. 159–60 Mr Kelly tries to get Kevin back. He's seen his mistake. Better than that, he *admits* it, and what's more, admits his need of and liking for Kevin. That all takes moral courage. Along with strong arms, Mr Kelly has strength of character.

Kate

Kate Kelly used to be Brede's friend and she fancies Kevin, but she loses both in this book. She makes a lot of mistakes: in fact you could plot her course through the book as a series of errors of navigation.

1. She fails to understand Brede's attitude to the violent children (p. 23).
2. She tries to chase Kevin (p. 75).
3. She gets involved with Brian (pp. 76, 116, 118).
4. She tries to defend Brian to Kevin (p. 116), and to cling on to Kevin (p. 117).
5. She bears false witness against Kevin (pp. 128–30).
6. She blames Brian for her treachery (p. 173).

Take a good look at these passages, and also pp. 24–6 (where Kate is mostly in the background, but says some revealing things). Now write a paragraph about Kate, saying *why* she makes mistakes. Is she:

stupid
lazy
evil
sexy
patriotic?

Is Kate another coward?

MR BLAKE

Mr Blake is a Protestant. He is a widower living alone – apart from his dog Jack – in a suburb of the city. He's a retired geography teacher who taught Sadie at school. He was known as Twinkle Blake because of his very bright blue eyes. He doesn't come into the story until Chapter 11.

There is no doubt that Mr Blake must have been a very good teacher; he has such a liking and understanding of young people. (At option choice time in his school, can't you imagine all the third-years choosing geography?)

Mr Blake may have made one very big mistake – far bigger than any made by anyone else in the novel. In Chapter 16 we learn about his anonymous letters and what he does with them. Pretend you are Mr

Blake trying to make up your mind what to do, and writing your thoughts in your private diary.

As yourself, write a statement comparing Mr Blake's death with the others in the novel (the dead civilian on p. 73, Mrs McConkey on pp. 99, 100 and 103) and saying how each affects you. Are all the deaths of the same significance? (Think in terms of morals as well as from the story point of view.)

THE HENDERSONS

Moira is a Catholic, Mike a Protestant. They are neighbours of Mr Blake's and have three children. Moira is a painter but has no time to paint any more. We are not told what Mike's job is.

Sadie loves Moira's paintings: to her they look 'vivid and exciting . . . alive' (p. 108). This is a good guide to the kind of person Moira is. She's also very ready to try Sadie's idea of child-minding because she's quick to see the value of new people and new ideas.

Mike is keen that Moira should get back to painting: in other words, he sees her as more than just a wife and mother, which is more than can be said for many husbands. He is very supportive to Sadie when he comes to break the news of Mr Blake's death.

The Hendersons have their problems: being partners in a mixed-religion marriage isn't easy, even if you're middle-class (see p. 109). Mike and Moira feel very nervous and edgy after Mr Blake's house has been bombed and they quarrel about what to do.

Write down what advice the Hendersons would have for Sadie and Kevin on how to cope with a 'mixed' relationship.

*

Joan Lingard was asked: *When you started with* The Twelfth Day of July, *did you know you were going to write a lot of books about those people?*
'No, I didn't. But at the end, when I left the main characters I found they were the kind that wouldn't lie down in my head, and I had to go on and find out what would happen to them next. Sometimes that

happens with characters, so there seemed little choice but to carry on and write *Across the Barricades*. I think when I got to the end of that I knew I would go on to *Into Exile*, because I could see I was going with them through this passage of their lives. So, in the end, I really go with them for seven years. Five books altogether.'

Did you ever get bored with Kevin and Sadie & Co.? Are they still lively for you?
'I think they stayed fairly lively because they're developing. I like to write books in which people are developing, changing. I think at the end of the book the chief characters should not be the same as they were at the opening. There's always a new stage in their life to explore.'

Themes

It is extremely difficult to write anything about Northern Ireland – fact or fiction – without sounding as though you are *for* one side and *against* the other. The difficulty increases if, like Joan Lingard, you are writing for young people and want to tell a really gripping story. She could put all the 'goodies' on one side (say Catholics) and the 'baddies' on the other (say Protestants). But she would then be in danger of convincing her many thousands of impressionable readers that all 'Micks' are angels and all 'Prods' are bent. Which would be (a) immoral, and (b) nonsense. So she has characters who are good, bad and in between on each side of the religious fence. She has to try her utmost to give all of them equal amounts of life and likelihood. To her it is worth the effort because the main theme of this book is:

THE STRUGGLE FOR TOLERATION

This is a world issue, not just a Northern Irish one, so you had better make sure that you know what toleration means. Tick any of the definitions here which you think are right.
Toleration is *passive*. It is:

- not taking much interest in political, religious or moral issues;
- letting everyone do their own thing without interfering with them:
- having your own ideas but not trying to make anyone agree with you;
- not arguing or fighting.

Toleration is *active*. It is:

- trying to understand people's ideas;
- trying to understand people's ideas even if you don't welcome them;
- recognizing people's right to think, speak and act as they want to.

The Chambers and Oxford Dictionaries define toleration as *giving liberty of expression* to minorities, *forbearing* to judge, *recognizing* rights: that's a thoughtful mixture of passive and active attitudes of mind. Something the dictionaries do not say, but which is equally true, is that if you have strong convictions or ideals of your own, achieving tolerance is difficult and showing tolerance does not make life easy.

This is what some of the characters in *Across the Barricades* find out. *Mr Blake's* commitment to toleration takes the most practical form; he offers help and refuge to a Protestant *and* a Catholic. But he is threatened and killed. *Kevin*, who steadily throughout the book becomes more and more sickened by bigotry,* is branded a coward if he expresses doubts about the value of violence. He then is trapped into violence himself by his own intolerance of treachery. *Sadie* escapes from Belfast with Kevin because she believes in their relationship, and it will only survive if they break away from the intolerance of both their upbringings. *Brede*, who believes as fervently in balance as most around her believe in prejudice, has lost a potential husband (Tommy) before the book begins, and then loses a friend (Kate) and a brother (Kevin). She must feel very isolated in her lonely bubble of toleration.

We get another view of the struggle by looking at the people who do not for one moment consider toleration – the bigots, in fact. They are principally *Brian* and *Steve*. And they can be summed up in two words: violent cowards. It is people like them who make the achievement of toleration such a struggle and so important.

It's dreadful to realize that Joan Lingard could have set her Kevin and Sadie books in so many other countries. Religious and/or political bigotry is part of the struggle for power in areas of every continent on earth. National news broadcasts highlight some of these struggles every day. Variations of Joan Lingard's story could equally well have

---

* Unreasoning and total attachment to a creed or viewpoint.

been set in Britain, where any number of violent/cowardly possibilities exist: sexual or racial hatreds, the animal liberation movement, the treatment of anti-nuclear protesters, etc. There is no doubt about it — you are studying a very serious book.

To back up your study, you should try to find out as much as you can about Northern Ireland. The sad and messy history of England's relationship with the big island to the west is very long: you should look not only at modern times but also at least as far back as the sixteenth century. You cannot do this properly without (a) help from school, and (b) remembering that however honourable historians and reporters are, it is very hard for them to be truly detached and a hundred per cent tolerant. Look at newspapers for information about conflicts in other parts of the world today.

Test yourself for toleration

Get into arguments and take part in debates. As you do so, try to observe yourself. Do you:

● *listen* to others?
● *take in* what they say?
● *believe* in their right to their opinions?
● *balance* your view of them accordingly?

Do *they* do any of these things when you spout your own opinions?

If you have firmly-held beliefs or theories, write them down as a sort of declaration. Get friends to do the same. Swap declarations and then each write what you think of them and of your friends who wrote them. Then swap back and discuss your reactions to each other. How much balance and toleration have you managed? Have you altered any of your relationships with your friends by doing this exercise? How difficult was it?

THE FAMILY

A very high proportion of the scenes in this book happen in the homes of the two main characters. This is not because Joan Lingard can't think of anywhere else to write about but because (a) Sadie and Kevin – restless through they may be – have very strong links with their families; and (b) their families have very strong motives for keeping Sadie and Kevin apart. In other words, each group of people, the Jacksons and the McCoys, becomes an important character in its own right.

The idea of the family as an important unit is tremendously strong in real life as well as in this book. The entire economic basis of Britain could be said to be 'the family', which is thought to produce well-motivated workers and eager, paying consumers of goods and services, generation after generation, *ad infinitum*. This is why politicians of all parties are always bringing 'the family' into their speeches and telling us that their legislation is good for 'the family'. But what is this family that politicians talk about? It seems to be a neat little household. The breadwinner – Dad – is married to Mum, who is usually doing un-waged work at home and a lot of shopping. Sometimes she goes out to work part-time for 'pin money'. Mum and Dad have two lovely kiddies.

Actually, only a small minority of families are like this. How many other kinds are there?

Does the word 'family' mean that there are bound to be children in the household? Could a single person living alone be called the smallest possible kind of family? What about two or more single people living together as friends or lovers, without children? What do you call a couple when their children have grown up and left home – a family?

We have come to something important here. Families spread about, don't they? You may have grandparents in Asia or the West Indies. Your sister might be 100 or 10,000 miles away. Your brother in the Forces could be posted anywhere. Kevin and Sadie escape *from home* at the end of the novel, but not *from their families*. This is because their and our ties of blood, affection and shared experience are so strong. Do you think that if Kevin or Sadie absolutely hated their families they could go away for good and say, 'I have *no* family'? Have you heard anyone say that? Are they freer or happier than you – or lonelier?

Background Information

A LITTLE GEOGRAPHY

Belfast is the capital of Northern Ireland. In June 1984 it had a population of about 327,000. (For comparison, Croydon had about 319,000; Coventry, 314,000; the Wirral, 337,500; Cardiff, 281,000; Edinburgh, 419,000.) About 27 per cent of the workforce was employed in manufacturing and construction. (The shipbuilding industry has diminished since Joan Lingard wrote *Across the Barricades* and had Mr Jackson and Tommy working in it.) Belfast has several parks. Bellevue Gardens and the adjoining grounds of Hazelwood form a park on the slopes of Cave Hill. The Zoological Gardens are there, and hillside and woodland walks. The River Lagan flows into Belfast Lough – a sea-lough. On the southern shore, in County Down, twelve miles from the city, you come to Bangor (see Chapters 7 and 18). This is Northern Ireland's fourth-largest town. It has four miles of seafront and is a favourite holiday centre. County Antrim, north of Belfast, is mountainous over a third of its area. This is where the glens are which Mr Blake, Sadie and Kevin were setting out for at the end of Chapter 16.

An Interesting Statistic

On the Northern Ireland census form in 1981 there was a question which did not *have* to be answered; it asked what was the religion of each person in every house. 18.5 per cent did not answer the question. (Of those who did, 414,532 were Catholic, over 1 million

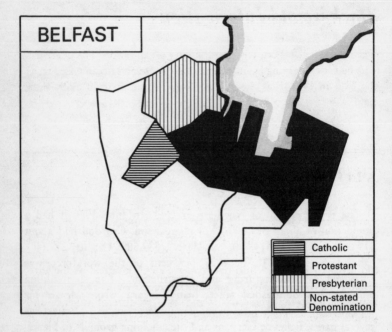

were Protestant of one kind or another, and nearly 59,000 were non-Christian.)

THE ORANGE ORDER

The Royal Orange Institution, to give it its proper name, is a semi-secret society. It is named after William III, who was of the House of Orange, but was founded in 1795, long after his reign. It has Lodges (branches) in the same way as the Masonic Order has. Its main objectives are the defence of the Protestant succession to the throne of Britain, and civil and religious liberty. In spite of this, the Orange Order does not fully agree with the idea of equal power-sharing between Catholics and Protestants, and it has attacked the civil rights movement, which it thinks is inspired by communists or by those who support the union of Southern and Northern Ireland.

THE IRISH REPUBLICAN ARMY

The IRA is a Southern Irish paramilitary organization. The guerrillas who had been fighting against the British in Ireland became known as the IRA in 1919. It is the military wing of the political party Sinn Fein.

THE PROVISIONAL IRA

In August 1969 there was serious fighting between Catholics and Protestants in Belfast, with a very bad outcome for the out-numbered Catholics. Some of them feared that British defence against Protestant extremism might not be reliable, and that the IRA was too involved in politics and not strong enough in arms; so the Pro-visional IRA was formed. Its members are known as Provos. Their aim is to unite the whole of Ireland by a mixture of violence and public demand. They have carried their violence into England at times.

SONGS

THE SASH MY FATHER WORE
(sung by Sadie, p. 59)

Sure I'm an Ulster Orange Man, from Erin's Isle I came,
To see my Glasgow Bretheren all of honour and of fame,
And to tell them of my forefathers who fought in days of yore –
All on the twelfth day of July in the sash me father wore.

Chorus:
It's ould but it's beautiful, it's the best you ever seen,
Been worn for more nor ninety years in that little Isle of Green.
From my Orange and Purple Forefather, it descended with galore –
It's a terror to them Papish boys, the sash me father wore.

So here I am in Glasgow town, youse boys and girls to see
And I hope that in good Orange style, you will welcome me,
A true blue blade that's just arrived from that dear Ulster shore –
All on the twelfth day of July in the sash me father wore.

Repeat Chorus:

And when I'm going to leave yeeze all, 'Good luck' till youse I'll say
And as I cross the raging sea, my Orange flute I'll play,
Returning to my native town, to ould Belfast once more,
To be welcomed back by Orangemen in the sash me father wore.

Repeat Chorus

(From *Soodlum's Selection of Irish Ballads*)

THE WEARING OF THE GREEN
(Sung by Kevin, p. 59)

O Paddy dear, and did you hear the news that's going round?
The Shamrock is by law forbid to grow on Irish ground;
St Patrick's Day no more we'll keep, his colours can't be seen,
For there's a bloody law again' the wearing of the green.
I met with Napper Tandy, and he took me by the hand,
And he said, 'How's poor old Ireland, and how does she stand?'
She's the most distressful country that ever yet was seen,
They are hanging men and women for the wearing of the green.

Then since the colour we must wear is England's cruel red,
Sure Ireland's sons will ne'er forget the blood that they have shed,
You may take the Shamrock from your hat, and cast it on the sod,
But 'twill take root and flourish there, though underfoot 'tis trod.
When law can stop the blades of grass from growing as they grow,
And when the leaves in summer time their verdure dare not show,
Then I will change the colour that I wear in my caubeen,
But till that day, please God, I'll stick to the wearing of the green.

But if at last our colour should be torn from Ireland's heart,
Her sons with shame and sorrow from the dear old isle will part;
I've heard a whisper of a country that lies beyond the sea,
Where rich and poor stand equal in the light of freedom's day.
O Erin, must we leave you, driven by a tyrant's hand?
Must we ask a mother's blessing from a strange and distant land?

Where the cruel cross of England shall never more be seen,
And where, please God, we'll live and die still wearing of the green.

(The version by Dion Boucicault of the
1798 original. From *Walton's New Treasury
of Irish Songs and Ballads*, Part 1)

Passages for Comparison

The writer Dervla Murphy has travelled widely – sometimes on a bicycle and sometimes with her young daughter – in many distant parts of the world. She comes from Southern Ireland, of a Catholic family, but has 'drifted away from the Church'. The book from which the first two passages are taken was originally published in 1978 but has been reprinted many times. It is an account of Dervla Murphy's travels on her bicycle in Northern Ireland. She was attempting to understand better the emotions aroused in herself and others by what is going on there.

The first passage will fill out for you some of the Protestant activities on 12 July every year.

At 9.10 a.m. I was introduced to the Loyal Orange Lodge that had adopted me for the day. It was a Primary – as distinct from District, County and Grand – Lodge in rather a 'deprived' area. Around the Orange Hall little tables were laden with beer bottles and whiskey glasses, and scrubbed-looking Orangemen, in their Sabbath suits, were drinking and smoking and quietly chatting. Each had his sash to hand, carefully wrapped in brown paper or plastic bag, and at the back of the Hall the first relay of banner-bearers were adjusting their leather harness and fixing bouquets of Sweet William and orange gladioli to the banner poles. I had scarcely crossed the threshold when I was being offered 'a wee one'. At the risk of seeming effete I chose beer. It was, as I had said, 9.10 a.m.

At 10.00 a.m. our Lodge moved off from the Hall . . . Since nine o'clock that air had been full of music and marching as Lodges from all over the city made their way to Carlisle Circus, the starting point for the procession of 299 Lodges and innumerable bands – including thirty from Scotland. At this stage I temporarily left 'my' Lodge, whose appointed place was near the end of the parade; I wanted to hurry ahead to reach a vantage point from which I could see the whole procession passing. For over an hour I walked fast through city centre streets lined with thousands upon thousands of cheerful citizens; and I found that even on pavements it is oddly untiring to walk to the beating of drums. Then the intense noon heat slowed up the proceedings and at a few points halts were called for ten minutes or so to give musicians and banner-bearers – not to mention all the aged stalwarts involved – a chance to refresh themselves with fizzy drinks or beer, depending on their devotion to Temperance . . .

These halts gave me a chance to overtake the leaders and by 1.30 I was sitting on a not too-crowded pavement on the Upper Malone Road next to a four-man UDR patrol who were lounging against their Land-Rover looking as though they wished that they too were marching.

Only then did I notice that the honour of leading the parade had been granted to the Dublin and Wicklow Loyal Orange Lodge. I felt quite proud to see my fellow-Southerners in this position – although I know very well their Orangeism may mean a somewhat lukewarm loyalty to the country of their residence. Most of the Dublin and Wicklow Orangemen were elderly if not downright ancient and their attire was impeccably traditional. They wore dark city suits, white shirts, bowler hats, Orange Order cuffs, white gloves and orange collarettes (The Sash) decorated with war medals and esoteric badges denoting the wearer's precise status within this semi-secret society. Many carried tightly rolled umbrellas as though they were bearing ceremonial swords and a few were solemnly shouldering silver-tipped pikes – perhaps in memory of the good old days before the Brits stood between them and the Papists. For the next hour and a half I watched hundreds of Loyal Orange Lodges passing; few were as correctly dressed as the Republic's representatives . . .

Each Lodge is ritually preceded by its banner and sometimes four strong men and a few small boys are required to cope with one banner – the boys holding its tasselled 'stays' lest the wind might take control. The gaily-coloured hand-painted pictures are often, I gather, of immense significance, yet many Loyal Orangemen are unable to explain why their particular banner depicts this or that . . .

The North supports more bands per head of the population than anywhere else in the UK . . . There are hundreds of bass drums, kettledrums, pipes, flutes, accordions, fifes, cymbals, trumpets – and the musicians are as varied as the instruments. I saw every type, age and size of person playing, from eight-year-old girls in thick blue woollen cardigans, white shirts and red skirts to seventy-five-year-old veterans in gorgeous scarlet uniforms with gold braiding . . .

To give a full description of this extraordinary spectacle would take up more pages than I have left at my disposal. It has often been called Europe's greatest folk-festival and today I could see why. I could also understand the grudging admiration and veiled pride with which many Northern Catholics refer to this essentially anti-Catholic demonstration. It is a magnificent event, unique to Northern Ireland, and they would hate to see it suppressed.

Every Orange march goes to a suitable field where most of the marchers collapse forthwith on the grass. The local leaders of the Order then make inflammatory speeches, and after an interval for rest, refreshment and relaxation the Lodges and bands reconstitute themselves and march back to their Orange Halls . . .

One can't all the time overlook the deeper implications of the Orangemen's festival because what is said from the platforms on the various Fields can be of crucial importance for Northern Ireland. True, I counted only 118 people out of some 40,000 listening to the speeches at Edenberry today. But the thousands who were not listening are, by the mere fact of being Orangemen, more or less amenable to the influence of their leaders when political crises arise. And today's speakers had the sort of minds that make even the Roman Curia seem progressive.

(From *A Place Apart* by Dervla Murphy, pp. 283–9)

The next passage, from the same book, is part of an account of a visit to a Catholic working-class area of Belfast which borders on a Protestant one.

I was advised to study the religious geography of the city before cycling around it and a friend lent me his detailed British Army Tribal Map of Belfast, which marks the ghetto areas orange and green. Then my host introduced me to the Catholic ghettos. With a prominent DOCTOR displayed on his windscreen he was less likely than other motorists to be delayed at security check-points, hijacked by bombers or stoned by gangs of bored boys who for the moment could find no more exciting target.

Perhaps because I never see television, and so was quite unprepared, those ghettoes really shattered me. Yet I have known far worse slums in Asia. But Belfast is in affluent Europe and why should large areas of it be swarming with under-nourished wild children and knee-deep in stinking litter, and strewn with broken glass glinting in hot sun under a blue sky – all on a summer's day . . . So many bricked-up houses, reminding me of dead people with their eyes shut – some of them fine substantial buildings from which Protestants had had to flee in terror taking only their resentment with them. So many high brick, or corrugated iron, barricades between identical streets of little working-class homes, to prevent neighbours seeing and hearing each other, and so being provoked to hurt and kill each other. Sometimes, over the barricades, I could glimpse Union Jacks flying from upstairs windows . . .

A filthy four- or five-year-old boy was playing all alone on a broken pavement with a length of stick; it was his gun and he was aiming at us. One wouldn't even notice him in London or Dublin but in Belfast I wondered, 'How soon will he have the real thing?' Already, in his little mind, possession of a gun is equated with bravery and safety, with having the will and ability to defend his own territory against 'the Oranges'. Around the next corner two slightly older children were carefully placing cardboard cartons in the middle of the narrow street. 'Are these pretend bombs?' I asked, appalled. 'They might not be pretend,' replied Jim, driving on the pavement to avoid one. Even more appalled, I said nothing. Jim looked at me and laughed. 'You'll get used to it!' he said. 'Almost certainly they are pretend. But hereabouts sensible people don't take chances.'

Everywhere stones and broken bricks were available to be thrown at passing army vehicles. Jagged broken bottles lay in gutters, flashing as they caught the strong sunlight. We passed an elaborately fortified barracks and then a famous 'confrontation spot'. 'In the afternoons,' explained Jim, 'you get the locals out here stoning the troops. And the same evening the same people will run across to the sentry-box and ask could they ever use the phone to ring the aunt in Armagh.'

When we took a wrong turning Jim became slightly tense. At the end of an artificial cul-de-sac – concrete-filled tar barrels were blocking the road to motor traffic – he turned quickly. A group of gum-chewing youths came sauntering round a corner and jeered at the posh car on principle. 'There's a wee bit of trouble on the way,' remarked Jim. 'It's funny, when you live here you develop a sixth sense – you always can tell when something's brewing.'

(pp. 121–2)

The last passage is from the 'Young Guardian' page of the *Guardian*, 11 March 1987.

A LESSON IN PEACE STUDIES
Denis Campbell on a brave experiment in breaking down sectarian barriers

'If every school in Northern Ireland was like ours there wouldn't be so much fighting.' So says Jonathan, a sixth-former at Belfast's Lagan College, the first fully integrated secondary school in Northern Ireland for both Catholics and Protestants.

Educating children of different religions together is normal in the rest of Britain. But in Northern Ireland – where 93 per cent of pupils are segregated in separate Catholic and Protestant schools – integrated education has been a daring, though very popular, experiment.

Lagan was set up by parents in the All Children Together reconcilation movement. They were alarmed that children in Northern Ireland only rarely meet across the religious divide. 'They see the other side as unknowns and they're suspicious. That creates barriers of mistrust and ignorance. They don't get the chance to know each other as people,' says Principal Mrs Sheila Greenfield.

The school opened in September, 1981 with twenty-eight first-year pupils and two teachers in a Scout hut.. It has added a new form a year. Today its 455 pupils, and twenty-eight teachers, occupy a redundant school on the Castlereagh hills overlooking Belfast.

Lagan's phenomenal success has proved that children of different religions can grow up happily together, and learn to respect each other, even when the world outside seems bitterly divided. And it has paved the way for other integrated schools in the Province – another secondary and three primaries have opened. Two more primary schools open this September.

For legal reasons Lagan was originally established as a private school but the Government now pays 85 per cent of its expenses and entry is open to everyone. Mrs Greenfield dismisses the idea that Lagan just attracts middle-class children. 'We've got pupils on free school meals, pupils whose parents are unemployed and pupils from the so-called ghettoes,' she says.

It was the first school in Northern Ireland to insist on an approximate 50/50, Catholic/Protestant, balance among pupils, staff and governors. Religious and ethnic identities are not concealed or flaunted. They are recognized, respected and discussed.

The curriculum stresses what is often overlooked about Northern Ireland . . . what the two communities have in common – their Christianity, history, language and literature . . . rather than what divides them.

A mixture of Irish and British Commonwealth history is taught, both the Battle of the Boyne and the Easter Rising.

Jonathan, John, Connor and Joanne were among Lagan's original twenty-eight pupils . . . 'the guinea pigs,' laughs Joanne. Barbara and Neil left other secondary schools to come to Lagan. All are in the sixth form.

'I've made lots of friends here from both religions. That wouldn't have happened if I'd gone to any other school,' says Jonathan. The others nod in agreement.

A worker for All Children Together said this in a letter to the writer of the Passnotes: 'We believe that parents have the fundamental right to choose the kind of education that should be given to their children and we are encouraged by the demand among parents in Northern Ireland to educate their children in planned, integrated schools. Integrated education is not designed to replace Protestant and Catholic schools, but rather to provide an alternative and additional system of education in N I. A C T are realists: we do not believe that integrated education will solve the N I problem but we do hope that it can break down some of the community tensions which exist in our country.'

Re-read the three passages above; think about the story of Sadie and Kevin's relationship; and then consider whether you think the last sentence in the quotation from the letter sounds

- realistic
- optimistic
- pessimistic

Look again at the passages from *A Place Apart*. They are examples of very good documentary writing. Do you think that material like this would fit into, improve or slow down the action in Joan Lingard's fictional writing? Do you think that she has succeeded in summing up the atmosphere of Belfast accurately and sufficiently? Before you write down your answer, bear in mind that:

- Dervla Murphy's book is not only documentary, it is for adults;
- Joan Lingard's book is not only fiction, it is for young readers;
- there's nothing to stop young readers trying to read Ms Murphy's book or adults trying to read Ms Lingard's.

Glossary

back-to-back   houses whose back doors face each other

the bit   the crunch

bletherer   chatterbox

Boyne   The River Boyne, where on 1 July 1690 the Protestant forces of William of Orange defeated the Catholic James II and thus completed the Protestant conquest of Ireland

boys   an exclamation such as 'My goodness!'

clodding   hurling with brute force

County Tyrone   west of Belfast and Lough Neagh

crack   natter

Curia   the Papal judicial court in the Vatican, Rome

da   dad

desperate   dreadful

digs   lodgings

dry bokes   retching

eejit   idiot

Fenian   abusive term for a Catholic

the 'Field' at Finaghy   a large open space in Belfast

fine well   very well

forby   as well

fried potato bread   a thin savoury scone mixture of flour, potato and water; can be eaten spread with butter or as part of a fry-up

fussy   bothered, concerned

garnished   decorated, embellished

gestating   being carried, and growing, in the womb

getting in the messages   doing the shopping

glens of Antrim   mountainous country north of Belfast

good crack   good company with good talk

hallion   tearaway

Insurance Day   every week or fortnight, the insurance man calls to collect instalments of household and/or personal insurance money

IRA   the Irish Republican Army

jar   a pint, a drink

King Billy William III

Labour Exchange old name for the place where unemployed people signed on and drew the dole or looked for jobs

lobby hall

Lough lake; pronounced as the Scottish 'loch'

Loyalist a term for Protestant Northern Irish people who are 'loyal' to the British crown

Mick abusive term for a Catholic

mitched played truant

mural painting on a wall

the night tonight

notion on to have a notion on someone is to fancy them

one Ireland many Catholics in the North and the South want Ireland to be reunited as one country

Orange Lodge the local branch of the Orange Order

Orangeman member of the Orange Order

Orange Order Protestant semi-secret society

Orange Walk massed march of Orangemen on 12 July

ould old

pieces sandwiches

Provos members of the Provisional I R A

rebels Catholics rebelling against the division of Ireland and against British rule in the North

Remember 1916 the Easter Rising in 1916 was meant to be a nationwide Catholic rebellion against British rule. In fact it hardly spread beyond Dublin and it ended in surrender and many executions

Republicans people loyal to the Irish Republic – i.e. Southern Ireland – or who want a united republican country

sarky sarcastic

sectarian belonging to a political or religious sect whose beliefs are not those of established and generally accepted bodies

Shannon a large river in Southern Ireland

Six Counties the counties which make up Northern Ireland: Fermanagh, Armagh, Down, Tyrone, Derry and Antrim

soda bread savoury scone about an inch thick; usually cut into triangles. The soda makes the bread rise

Specials the 'B' Specials were a paramilitary Protestant body which became extremely unpopular. They no longer exist

stance bus-stop stand

stool pigeon person acting as a decoy or bait

Taig abusive term for a Catholic

UDR   the Ulster Defence Regiment; a part of the British army. It has both
   Catholic and Protestant members, but Catholic membership is small
waiting on   waiting for
wee   small
white slave traffic   the abduction of young white women to be sold abroad
   for the purposes of male sexual pleasure
yet   still
youse   plural of you

FOR THE BEST IN PAPERBACKS, LOOK FOR THE

In every corner of the world, on every subject under the sun, Penguin represents quality and variety – the very best in publishing today.

For complete information about books available from Penguin – including Pelicans, Puffins, Peregrines and Penguin Classics – and how to order them, write to us at the appropriate address below. Please note that for copyright reasons the selection of books varies from country to country.

In the United Kingdom: For a complete list of books available from Penguin in the U.K., please write to *Dept E.P., Penguin Books Ltd, Harmondsworth, Middlesex, UB7 0DA*

In the United States: For a complete list of books available from Penguin in the U.S., please write to *Dept BA, Penguin, 299 Murray Hill Parkway, East Rutherford, New Jersey 07073*

In Canada: For a complete list of books available from Penguin in Canada, please write to *Penguin Books Canada Ltd, 2801 John Street, Markham, Ontario L3R 1B4*

In Australia: For a complete list of books available from Penguin in Australia, please write to the *Marketing Department, Penguin Books Australia Ltd, P.O. Box 257, Ringwood, Victoria 3134*

In New Zealand: For a complete list of books available from Penguin in New Zealand, please write to the *Marketing Department, Penguin Books (NZ) Ltd, Private Bag, Takapuna, Auckland 9*

In India: For a complete list of books available from Penguin, please write to *Penguin Overseas Ltd, 706 Eros Apartments, 56 Nehru Place, New Delhi, 110019*

In Holland: For a complete list of books available from Penguin in Holland, please write to *Penguin Books Nederland B.V., Postbus 195, NL–1380AD Weesp, Netherlands*

In Germany: For a complete list of books available from Penguin, please write to *Penguin Books Ltd, Friedrichstrasse 10 – 12, D–6000 Frankfurt Main 1, Federal Republic of Germany*

In Spain: For a complete list of books available from Penguin in Spain, please write to *Longman Penguin España, Calle San Nicolas 15, E–28013 Madrid, Spain*

FOR THE BEST IN PAPERBACKS, LOOK FOR THE

PENGUIN CLASSICS

Netochka Nezvanova   Fyodor Dostoyevsky

Dostoyevsky's first book tells the story of 'Nameless Nobody' and introduces many of the themes and issues which will dominate his great masterpieces.

Selections from the Carmina Burana   A verse translation by David Parlett

The famous songs from the *Carmina Burana* (made into an oratorio by Carl Orff) tell of lecherous monks and corrupt clerics, drinkers and gamblers, and the fleeting pleasures of youth.

Fear and Trembling   Søren Kierkegaard

A profound meditation on the nature of faith and submission to God's will which examines with startling originality the story of Abraham and Isaac.

Selected Prose   Charles Lamb

Lamb's famous essays (under the strange pseudonym of Elia) on anything and everything have long been celebrated for their apparently innocent charm; this major new edition allows readers to discover the darker and more interesting aspects of Lamb.

The Picture of Dorian Gray   Oscar Wilde

Wilde's superb and macabre novella, one of his supreme works, is reprinted here with a masterly Introduction and valuable Notes by Peter Ackroyd.

A Treatise of Human Nature   David Hume

A universally acknowledged masterpiece by 'the greatest of all British Philosophers' – A. J. Ayer

FOR THE BEST IN PAPERBACKS, LOOK FOR THE

PENGUIN CLASSICS

A Passage to India E. M. Forster

Centred on the unresolved mystery in the Marabar Caves, Forster's great work provides the definitive evocation of the British Raj.

The Republic Plato

The best-known of Plato's dialogues, *The Republic* is also one of the supreme masterpieces of Western philosophy whose influence cannot be overestimated.

The Life of Johnson James Boswell

Perhaps the finest 'life' ever written, Boswell's *Johnson* captures for all time one of the most colourful and talented figures in English literary history.

Remembrance of Things Past (3 volumes) Marcel Proust

This revised version by Terence Kilmartin of C. K. Scott Moncrieff's original translation has been universally acclaimed – available for the first time in paperback.

Metamorphoses Ovid

A golden treasury of myths and legends which has proved a major influence on Western literature.

A Nietzsche Reader Friedrich Nietzsche

A superb selection from all the major works of one of the greatest thinkers and writers in world literature, translated into clear, modern English.

Matthew Arnold	**Selected Prose**
Jane Austen	**Emma**
	Lady Susan, The Watsons, Sanditon
	Mansfield Park
	Northanger Abbey
	Persuasion
	Pride and Prejudice
	Sense and Sensibility
Anne Brontë	**The Tenant of Wildfell Hall**
Charlotte Brontë	**Jane Eyre**
	Shirley
	Villette
Emily Brontë	**Wuthering Heights**
Samuel Butler	**Erewhon**
	The Way of All Flesh
Thomas Carlyle	**Selected Writings**
Wilkie Collins	**The Moonstone**
	The Woman in White
Charles Darwin	**The Origin of Species**
Charles Dickens	**American Notes for General Circulation**
	Barnaby Rudge
	Bleak House
	The Christmas Books
	David Copperfield
	Dombey and Son
	Great Expectations
	Hard Times
	Little Dorrit
	Martin Chuzzlewit
	The Mystery of Edwin Drood
	Nicholas Nickleby
	The Old Curiosity Shop
	Oliver Twist
	Our Mutual Friend
	The Pickwick Papers
	Selected Short Fiction
	A Tale of Two Cities

FOR THE BEST IN PAPERBACKS, LOOK FOR THE

PENGUIN MASTERSTUDIES

This comprehensive list, designed for advanced level and first-year under-graduate studies, includes:

SUBJECTS
Applied Mathematics
Biology
Drama: Text into Performance
Geography
Pure Mathematics

LITERATURE
Absalom and Achitophel
Barchester Towers
Dr Faustus
Eugénie Grandet
The Great Gatsby
Gulliver's Travels
Joseph Andrews
The Mill on the Floss
A Passage to India
Persuasion *and* Emma
Portrait of a Lady
Tender Is the Night
Vanity Fair
The Waste Land

CHAUCER
The Knight's Tale
The Miller's Tale
The Nun's Priest's Tale
The Pardoner's Tale
The Prologue to The Canterbury
   Tales
A Chaucer Handbook

SHAKESPEARE
Antony & Cleopatra
Hamlet
King Lear
Measure for Measure
Much Ado About Nothing
Othello
The Tempest
A Shakespeare Handbook

'Standing somewhere between the literal, word-by-word explication of more usual notes and the abstractions of an academic monograph, the Masterstudies series is an admirable introduction to mainstream literary criticism for A Level students, in particular for those contemplating reading English at university. More than that, it is also a model of what student notes can achieve' – *The Times Literary Supplement*

FOR THE BEST IN PAPERBACKS, LOOK FOR THE

PENGUIN PASSNOTES

This comprehensive series, designed to help O-level, GCSE and CSE students, includes:

SUBJECTS
Biology
Chemistry
Economics
English Language
Geography
Human Biology
Mathematics
Modern Mathematics
Modern World History
Narrative Poems
Nursing
Physics

SHAKESPEARE
As You Like It
Henry IV, Part I
Henry V
Julius Caesar
Macbeth
The Merchant of Venice
A Midsummer Night's Dream
Romeo and Juliet
Twelfth Night

LITERATURE
Arms and the Man
Cider With Rosie
Great Expectations
Jane Eyre
Kes
Lord of the Flies
A Man for All Seasons
The Mayor of Casterbridge
My Family and Other Animals
Pride and Prejudice
The Prologue to The Canterbury
    Tales
Pygmalion
Saint Joan
She Stoops to Conquer
Silas Marner
To Kill a Mockingbird
War of the Worlds
The Woman in White
Wuthering Heights